In further axed DC comics movie news, during an interview with Collider, writer Akiva Goldsman revealed new information on the early 2000's version of *Batman vs. Superman*. This one was intended to be directed by Wolfgang Peterson and star Colin Farrel as Batman and Jude Law as Superman. For those who thought that 2015's *Batman v Superman* was too dark, Goldsman said his version was "the darkest thing you've ever seen."

The movie would have opened with Bruce Wayne attending Alfred's funeral. With him is his wife. Bruce has apparently given up being Batman and leads a happily married life... until the Joker murders her. Then, it turns out that the Joker orchestrated the whole romance to begin with to break Batman!

Superman, meanwhile, has recently divorced Lois Lane and has begun a romance with Lana Lang. Despite the proposed film's title, the duo would start the movie as already being friends (Clark would be the best man at Bruce's wedding).

Eventually, Bruce puts back on the cowl and he and Supes must find a way to defeat Lex Luthor and the Joker.

If you're interested in more details, Goldsman was interviewed recently on the Collider Connected podcast.

NEWS BRIEFS

NEW BRUCE LEE SET FROM CRITERION On July 14, 2020, Criterion will release Bruce Lee's Greatest Hits. The set contains all the films you'd expect, including *The Big Boss, Fist of Fury, The Way of the Dragon, Enter the Dragon*, and *Game of Death*.

This set will be of interest to lost film aficionados because it contains the new feature *Game of Death Redux*, "a new presentation of Lee's original *Game of Death* footage, produced by Alan Canvan."

Game of Death started shooting before Lee was offered *Enter the Dragon*. He suspended filming before the movie was finished to do *Enter the Dragon*. Lee passed away before resuming work on *Game of Death*, and so the film was released in the fashion of *Trail of the Pink Panther*, making a new storyline out of the late star's existing footage. Hopefully the new feature will shed some more light on what could have been.

Godzilla is a registered TM © Toho Co., Ltd.

Franco Nero in *Django Strikes Again* (1986).

NEW GODZILLA MOVIE...BUT ONLY IN JAPAN The good news: a new official Godzilla movie (albeit a short one) has been released in Japan. The bad news: you can ONLY see it in Japan. Godzilla Appears in Sukagawa　(ゴジラ須賀川に現) was produced specifically for the Eiji Tsuburaya Museum in Sukagawa, and as of right now that's the only place one can view it. The short film features an exact replica of the 1954 Godzilla suit attacking Sukagawa. Here's to hoping one day Toho sees fit to release it in some capacity for Godzilla fans unable to view it in Japan.

NO NEWS IS GOOD NEWS? No updates on *Grizzly II: Revenge* other than that sometime in 2020 it will receive a DVD/Blu-Ray/VOD release. The same goes for David Allen's *The Primevals*, another lost film in the process of being completed.

DEVELOPMENT HELL

DJANGO LIVES Four years ago, it was announced that the original *Piranha* writer John Sayles would write *Django Lives*, with Franco Nero reprising the role that made him famous.

The film was shopped around at Cannes in 2017. The plan was for the film to be shot in Spain and Berlin, Germany. The slated director was Christian Alvart, who named one of his sons Django.

The proposed storyline would have Django fighting white supremacists in 1914 America. Other reports also mentioned that Django would find himself working in the early days of Motion Pictures on Westerns. For now all is quiet on the western front regarding *Django Lives*, hopefully it does.

KOSEIDON China's Tencent Pictures announced their adaptation of the Tsuburaya Productions 1970's era TV series *Dinosaur Task Force Koseidon* in 2016. Is it still quietly in development, or dead in the water?

UNTITLED WEREWOLF WESTERN Guillermo Del Torro has a werewolf western in the works that sounds too good to be true for genre lovers. If all goes well Del Toro will produce and Issa López (*Tigers Are Not Afraid*) will direct. Here's hoping that it doesn't become one of those tantalizing lost projects you read about in a magazine a long, long time ago...

THE LOST FILMS FANZINE

EDITORIAL

THE LOST FILMS FANZINE, VOL. 1, #2 SUMMER 2020

EDITOR AND PUBLISHER: JOHN LEMAY
SPECIAL CONSULTANT: KYLE BYRD
SPECIAL THANKS THIS ISSUE TO CONNOR ANDERSON

THE LOST FILMS FANZINE IS PUBLISHED FOUR TIMES A YEAR. THE COPYRIGHTS AND TRADEMARKS OF THE IMAGES FEATURED THEREIN ARE HELD BY THEIR RESPECTIVE OWNERS. THE LOST FILMS FANZINE ACKNOWLEDGES THE RIGHTS OF THE CREATORS AND THE COPYRIGHT HOLDERS OF THE IMAGES THEREIN AND DOES NOT SEEK TO INFRINGE UPON THOSE RIGHTS. IMAGES USED HEREIN ARE PUBLICITY IMAGES AND ARE USED IN THE INTEREST OF EDUCATION AND PUBLICITY. ARTICLES AND TEXT WITHIN THE MAGAZINE ARE © THEIR RESPECTIVE AUTHORS AND MAY NOT BE REPRINTED WITHOUT PERMISSION. FRONT COVER (COLOR VERSION), MAIN IMAGE: TARZAN ESCAPES © MGM 1936. TARZAN IS A REGISTERED TM OF EDGAR RICE BURROUGHS, INC. ALL RIGHTS RESERVED. FRONT COVER (B&W VERSION), MAIN IMAGE: ORCA © 1977 DINO DE LAURENTIIS COMPANY.

It was a little over a year ago that I had the pleasure of meeting artist Christopher Martinez. A friend of mine, Greg Noneman, had commissioned artwork from several artists in relation to a panel we were doing on Hammer and Toho's unmade *Nessie* movie for G-Fest in 2019. I was also at the time working to revise and update *The Big Book of Japanese Giant Monster Movies: The Lost Films*. I wanted to give it a retro look, like a paperback from the 1960s. When I saw Chris's artwork for *Nessie*, it struck a chord with me. It would be the perfect cover. I asked him about purchasing the artwork for the cover, and Chris, being the nice guy that he was, barely charged me a dime for it.

I loved Chris's style so much I hired him to do the covers for a whole series I was doing on ufology and cryptozoology in the Old West (*Cowboys & Saurians* and *The Real Cowboys & Aliens* with Noe Torres). He and I had a blast talking different concept ideas for covers (I had about ten books in mind for the series). Our creative minds were certainly on the same wavelength, which is rare.

I had hoped that Chris and I would have many years together of collaboration and friendship, but this spring Chris passed away. He had been fighting cancer for the past two years. Things were looking better for him when I saw him at G-Fest, but in the winter months of 2020, his health tragically took a turn for the worst.

I will miss talking to you Chris, you were one of the nicest, most un-selfish, talented, and easy to work with creators in this whole community. Rest in peace my friend.

John LeMay

NEWS

Joe Manganiello as Deathstroke in *Justice League* (2017). © Warner Bros./DC Comics

DEATHSTROKE UNMADE

With interest in unmade movies on the rise, today's filmmakers are becoming more talkative as to their original plans and ideas for various projects. As we all know, the less than stellar reaction to 2017's *Justice League* movie shook up the future of the DC cinematic universe. One of the better received aspects of the movie was a tag scene featuring Joe Manganiello as Deathstroke.

Initially, Warner Bros wanted a *Deathstroke* spinoff movie and approached *The Raid* director Gareth Evans about directing. Refreshingly, Evans said that he didn't want to do another bloated, overstuffed superhero movie and wanted to specifically make something that clocked in at under two hours for a change.

Evans said he had plans for a Shakespearian origin story and that his style for the proposed film would have been noir films out of South Korea. "The texture, and the tones of colours, the grit and the aggression of them is super interesting to use to tell Deathstroke's story," he told superherohype.com.

Though he's aware that the project is most likely dead for good, Evans also said, "They might come back again in five or ten years time, you never know."

This isn't as far out as you may think. Steven Spielberg has been planning a Blackhawks movie (a DC property about WWII era ace pilots) since the early 1980s, and it's only just now looking to get made. (Or, at least, an announcement was made to that effect in 2018, who knows if it ever will get made).

SUPERMAN V:
THE QUEST FOR A NEW MOVIE

Superman © DC Comics/Time Warner and the heirs of Superman co-creator, Jerry Siegel

IN THE LATE 1970s, *Superman: The Movie* helped to create the modern "blockbuster" along with *Star Wars* and *Jaws*. And though it had some production problems, *Superman II* was also a big hit when released in 1980.

The trouble for the Christopher Reeve era Superman franchise probably started back in 1983 with *Superman III*. Although financially successful, it was not well-received and mostly rode on the coattails of the more popular *Superman II*. Making matters worse was the disastrous release of *Supergirl* in 1984, which was neither a critical or financial success. The Salkinds, who had produced the four aforementioned films, sold the Superman rights to Cannon Films in 1986. Production on a fourth Superman film began that same year, with Reeve coming back mostly because he had come up with the story pitch (that of Superman trying to rid the world of nuclear weapons).

Cannon was headed by Menahem Golan and Yoram Globus—known collectively as, what else, Golan-Globus—who were notoriously cheap producers. *Superman IV: The Quest for Peace*, was one of over 30 projects the studio was developing at the time and received no real special consideration. Cannon was given around $34 million by Warner Bros to help finance the film, but Cannon only put about half that into the picture and dispersed the rest to other projects!

The special effects scenes suffered the most and were noticeably below the quality of *Superman III*. As such, some of the cast and crew went so far as to consider the film being "unfinished" when it was finally released. The film debuted at #4 at the U.S. box office in late July of 1987. By week three, the film was out of the top ten all together and only grossed $15,681,020 total.

And yet, Cannon was still thinking about *Superman V*. Only three months later they announced the film via a brochure given out at the 1988 Cannes Film Festival. Rumors at the time suggested Albert Pyun would direct with hopes of getting it out by the Summer of 1989. Cheapos that they were, Cannon

Superman IV: The Quest for Peace © 1987 DC Comics/Time Warner

One of many stills to show Clark and Lacy at a Metropolis nightclub.

was looking to base the new film around 45 minutes' worth of cut footage from *Superman IV*!

What had happened was that the original cut of *Superman IV* clocked in at 134 minutes. However, an ill-received test screening in Orange County, California, convinced Cannon to cut the film down to 90 minutes. This would also allow theaters to show the movie more times during the day. To add insult to injury, supposedly, the film's editor, John Shirley, was instructed to destroy the 45 minutes' worth of extraneous footage. This is unlikely, though, as some of the deleted scenes have surfaced on DVD and Blu-Ray releases. (And, if it was destroyed, how could Cannon consider it for *Superman V*?)

It's debatable story-wise how much of the cut-footage would have been usable. The main centerpiece had Clark Kent going on a date with Lacy Warfield. While the duo is at a nightclub, Nuclear Man #1 comes knocking.

You see, Mark Pillow's character is actually Nuclear Man #2. Lex Luthor had created a proto-version of the

character. Nuclear Man #1 was played by Clive Mantle, and had a Frankenstein-like quality to him. Some might even compare him to Bizzaro... which is what he was initially. Reeve had the idea that the character would be Bizzaro and that he would play him, but producers deemed it too complicated, and the idea was dropped. So the character simply inherited Bizzaro's traits instead.

The nightclub scene began with Clark and Lacy bribing their way into the club, although Clark feels bad for a young couple that wasn't able to get in themselves. Inside, Clark Kent bumbles around like Clark Kent does, and another man takes Lacy out onto the dance floor. Clark then uses his superpowers to whisk the young couple he felt sorry for inside in a funny little scene.

Then in walks Nuclear Man #1, and it's love at first sight when he sees Lacy. (You see, Nuclear Man #2 has all of #1's memories, hence why he becomes obsessed with Lacy). He bumbles his way through the club, causing a man to spill his drink. The man then attempts to punch

Superman IV: The Quest for Peace © 1987 DC Comics/Time Warner

Clive Mantle as Nuclear Man #1 in the club (left) and with Gene Hackman (above).

Nuclear Man strikes first, sending Superman sailing past a well-placed Burger King. Nuclear Man shakes his fist in pain; it's the first time he ever hit something that hurt him. When Superman goes to hit him, Nuclear Man throws him through the air and then makes a comical flying motion with his hands.

Nuclear Man tries to push a row of parked cars into the Man of Steel. The two supermen then test their strength against one another, each pushing against their respective end of the train of cars until they are all crushed. Superman finally lands a hit on Nuclear Man and sends him flying.

Nuclear Man makes a chicken-like motion with his elbows and hops onto a rooftop. Superman gets it by now that he's fighting a dumb brute that is semi-innocent and tries to make peace with him. Luthor's command to "Destroy Superman!" echoes in Nuclear Man's brain, and he punches Supes through a Burger King billboard and into a passing semi-truck trailer.

Nuclear Man uproots a streetlight and attempts to hit Superman with it, but Supes grabs the other end and butts it into Nuclear Man. The

Nuclear Man, but he grabs his hand and crushes it. Nuclear Man is stopped before he can get to Lacy by what we would today call a "cougar." The older woman, enthralled by the muscular Nuclear Man, leads him outside to where they can be alone.

Now, none of what I just described has ever surfaced as deleted footage, but it was most certainly filmed as stills exist of the scene (and it appeared in the novelization). For whatever reason, it's simply among the lost footage.

Now, onto the footage that you can see. It shows the woman and Nuclear Man outside, where she unbuttons his shirt. To her horror, electricity generates from his scarred chest. She runs away screaming while Superman walks out of the club.

second-rate Bizzaro rip-off sails through the air and hits an electrical grid, causing him to explode.

And why exactly would Cannon write a whole movie around getting to use this less than five minute scene? Because it cost them $6 million, that's why! While this footage certainly could have been used, I wonder if they would have brought back the Lacey Warfield character. As it was, Margot Kidder barely returned for #4, nor was she happy with the results. So a love interest besides Kidder would probably have been needed for *Superman V* anyway. So there is a good possibility that the character would have been brought back, in this case, so the duo could "rekindle" their romance perhaps.

The other deleted scenes were not as exciting, and many of them tied directly into plot threads applicable only to *Superman IV*, such as Superman flying Jeremy (the kid who wrote him the letter) around the world, etc.

Furthermore, for all we know, Cannon might have used the Nuclear Man scene as a teaser scene to kick off the movie. Or, maybe they even had ideas of Gene Hackman's Luthor creating a "second" Nuclear Man in Part V. Who knows?

Superman goes green for £5m

SUPERMAN star Christopher Reeve has been made a £5million offer he cannot refuse to play the hero in a "green" movie.

The plot has Superman battling to save the earth's protective ozone layer.

Reeve, 37, vowed to hang up his blue tights last month because he was bored with the role.

But sources at London's Pinewood Studios say the money was too good to resist and he has agreed to play the super hero for a fifth time.

An insider claimed: "It would be impossible for audiences to accept a new actor."

Superman IV: The Quest for Peace © 1987 DC Comics/Time Warner

As it is, the story details are unknown other than that the plot would be written to accommodate the deleted footage. The only indication I can find regarding plot details are via a mysterious, undated newspaper article that reads:

Superman star Christopher Reeve has been made a £5million offer he cannot refuse to play the hero in a "green" movie.

The plot has Superman battling to save the earth's protective ozone layer.

Reeve, 37, vowed to hang up his blue tights last month because he was bored with the role.

But sources at London's Pinewood Studios say the money was too good to resist and he has agreed to play the super hero for a fifth time.

An insider claimed: "It would be impossible for audiences to accept a new actor."

Word on the street is that Reeve did indeed meet with Cannon about *Superman V*, and this time he would direct (though this conflicts with other sources stating that Albert

Superman V announcement handed out at the Cannes Film Festival in 1988.

Pyun would direct). But, Reeve eventually gave up on the idea, probably realizing that Cannon didn't have the finances to do a fifth film justice. Cannon, in turn, considered using a different actor.

But, during the time of *Superman V*'s development, Cannon was in the middle of a shakeup. None of their recent efforts had proved to be the big hits they anticipated—1987's *Masters of the Universe* chief among them along with *Superman IV*. Cannon was soon after taken over by Pathé Communications and Menahem Golan left the company.

After this, the rights lapsed back into the hand of the Salkinds, who had actually only leased the rights to Cannon for a limited time. It is at this point in the chronology that things get murky as they so often do in regards to cancelled films.

According to a chapter entitled "Superman Returns... Eventually (Part I)" in the book *Uncle John's Triumphant 20th Anniversary Bathroom Reader*, the original plan

and agreement between Cannon and the Salkinds went like this. Cannon would have the rights to Superman up until the point that they either made a fifth Superman or passed on it. Cannon's plan was not only to do *Superman V*, comprised of "two-thirds" of a deleted subplot from *Superman IV,* according to the *Bathroom Reader*, but also a *Superman VI* directed by Reeve. According to the sequence of events put forth in the *Bathroom Reader*, Reeve backed out of filming the additional scenes needed to complete Part V, which therefore negated part VI entirely. When that happened, the rights reverted to the Salkinds.

Our next questions is, after the Salkinds lost faith in the Superman franchise after *Supergirl*, what made them want it back— especially in light of *Superman IV's* failure? The answer lies in the fact that the Salkinds had begotten a *Superboy* T.V. series in the interim (later retitled *The Adventures of*

The Adventures of Superboy © 1989 DC Comics/Time Warner

Gerard Christopher as Superboy.

Batman became a huge hit, so perhaps the Salkinds also took note of that.

The Salkinds were thinking about doing a new movie, which was literally to be titled *Superman: The New Movie.* Coincidentally, one of the *Superboy* writers, Cary Bates, had written a spec story for a fifth Superman movie on a whim. He showed the treatment to Ilya Salkind, unaware that the Salkinds were already pondering a fifth Superman movie.[1] The Salkinds liked the idea, which wasn't surprising. As it was, Bates's idea was very close to Salkind's original plan for *Superman III,* which had Brainiac as the villain.

The plot for *The New Movie,* which Bates called *Superman V: Superman Reborn,* would ignore *Superman III* and *IV,* and pick up where *II* left off (with Lois pregnant with Superman's child according to some reports). Brainiac comes to Earth and shrinks Metropolis a la' the bottled city of Kandor with Superman still in it. Brainiac becomes aware that a super powered Kryptonian lurks within the shrunken Metropolis. Brainiac shrinks himself down to size and enters the city to investigate. He and Superman fight and the Man of Steel appears to die. But, because Metropolis is right next door to the Kryptonian city of Kandor in Brainiac's collection, Superman's molecules somehow reassemble in Kandor. There Superman reforms as a normal, mortal man (Kandor

Superboy). The series debuted straight to syndication in 1988 and initially starred John Haymes Newton before he was replaced by Gerard Christopher for the second season. In 1989, Tim Burton's

Superman © DC Comics/Time Warner and the heirs of Superman co-creator, Jerry Siegel

lacks the Earth's yellow sun, remember). Eventually Superman manages to get back to Metropolis, where he regains his powers and defeats Braniac. Though a tad repetitive of *Superman II*, it still would have been a better sendoff for Reeve than *Superman IV*. If Reeve was to star, that is.

Conflicting sources state that the Salkinds approached Reeve who declined, while others act as though they went straight for *Superboy* star Gerard Christopher.

As for other rumors in the mill that can't be verified, it's also whispered that Mr. Mxyzptlk would have been a side villain alongside Braniac. It's also rumored the movie would have been shot in the same location as the Superboy T.V. series in Florida.

This begs the question: would Gerard Christopher's incarnation be a continuation of his Superboy character now all grown up? Or, if not, would the movie have some loose ties to *Superman II*? Or would it be its own continuity altogether?

The hope was to get the film before cameras by late 1990 for a release during Christmas of 1991. Supposedly the budget was set between $35 and $40 million.

Whatever *Superman V: The New Movie* may or may not have entailed, the Salkinds' rights expired in 1992, and Superman was entirely back in the hands of Warner Bros. However, Bates was hired by Warner Bros to do a second draft of the story, which will be covered in a later issue...

---

[1] Supposedly the Salkinds had ideas of a *Superboy* movie as far back as season one. This is evidenced by the first Superboy, John Haymes Newton, stating that there was a possibility of him playing Superman on the big screen too. Fans then codenamed this potential film *Young Superman*.

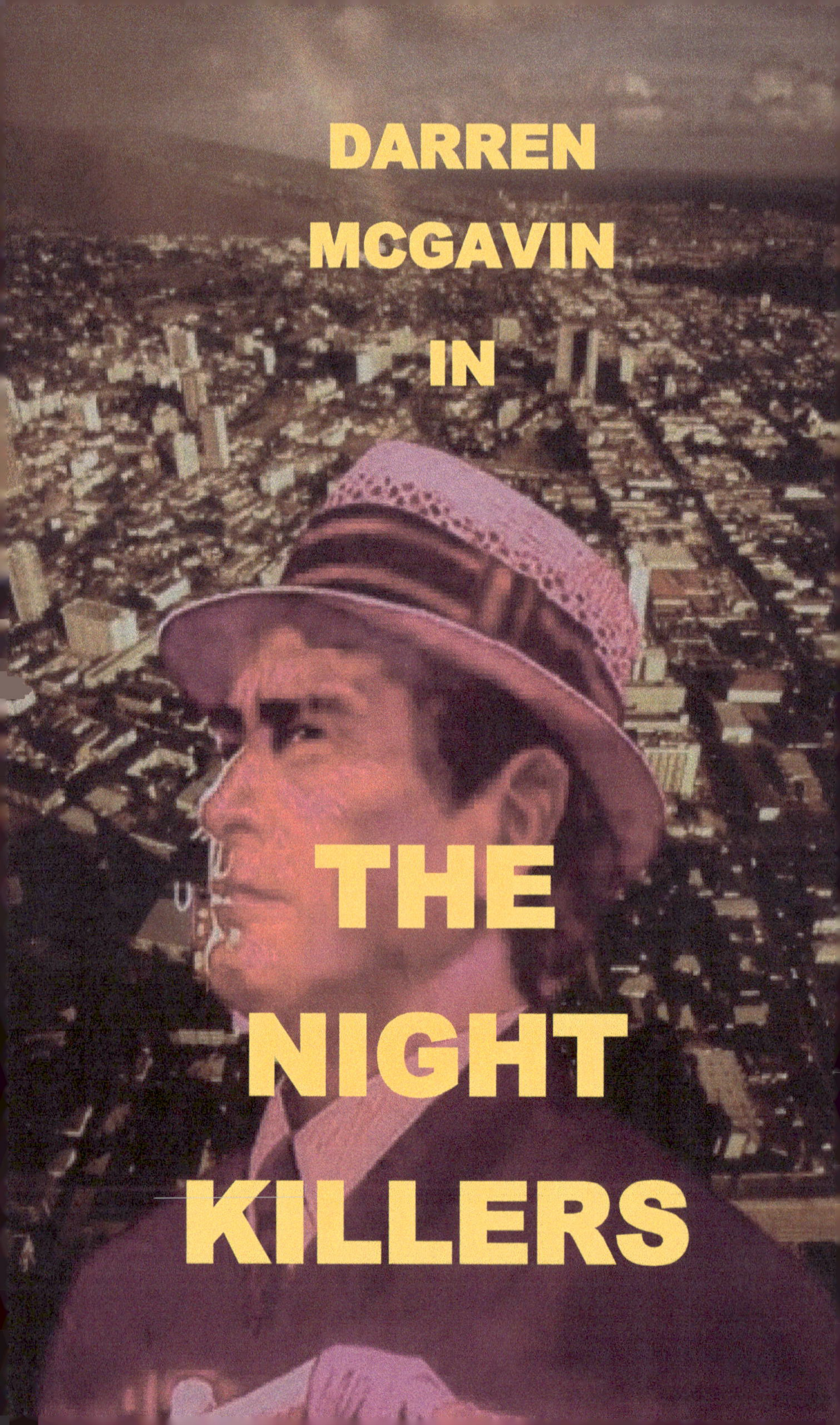

DARREN McGAVIN

IN

THE NIGHT KILLERS

Kolchak: The Night Stalker © 1974 Universal Television

KOLCHAK'S LOST MOVIES

On January 11, 1972, ABC aired another of their "Movies of the Week." This one was produced by *Dark Shadows* creator Dan Curtis and was about a reporter chasing down a modern-day vampire in Las Vegas. It was based upon an unpublished novel, *The Kolchak Papers*, by Jeff Rice and was renamed *The Night Stalker* for TV. To ABC's surprise, the movie was a huge hit. Not just that, it was the highest rated TV movie ever broadcast, securing a 33.2 rating. As such, the film was released theatrically in other countries, and naturally spawned a sequel, *The Night Strangler*, in 1973. As we all know, this was then followed by a TV series in 1974 called *Kolchak: The Night Stalker*.

But that wasn't always the plan. Steve Gentry, ABC's new vice president (and also the man in

13

Kolchak talks to an android in the episode called "Mr. R.I.N.G." Kolchak: The Night Stalker © 1974 Universal Television

As to the chance that McGavin may not return, there were several ideas at play. For starters, ABC was already thinking of a long term game plan to keep Kolchak going. The thought was either that movie #3 could serve as a TV series pilot, or it could be the start of a once-a-month TV movie or mini-series starring Kolchak. Furthermore, if McGavin wouldn't return for the third movie, ABC would simply recast the part. If the movie was another hit, ABC would see that like James Bond, Kolchak could simply be recast and that it was the character itself, not the actor, that audiences connected with.

Another problem was that Matheson was quite busy at the time, too busy, he felt, to give the script enough attention. So Matheson invited his friend and *Logan's Run* writer William F. Nolan to write the script. Nolan accepted and finished a first draft by January 15, 1974.

Matheson was quite happy with the script, called *The Night Killers* (clearly they were running low on interesting adjectives by then). "I don't know why they didn't go ahead with it. It was a neat premise for the time."[2]

The premise Matheson spoke of was aliens—specifically aliens landing in Hawaii and replacing high-level authorities with robotic doubles.

Though Matheson liked it, most Kolchak fans that have read it agree that had it been produced, a TV

charge of TV movies) was happy with *Night Strangler's* ratings and asked Curtis for a third Kolchak movie. There was one problem though, Curtis and the man who played Kolchak, Darren McGavin, were currently on the outs. Still, Curtis decided to call up the original movie's writer, Richard Matheson, about doing another. Never mind that Kolchak's creator, Jeff Rice, had approached ABC about writing a third movie right after *Night Strangler* aired. (Though I don't know the premise of his story, I know the setting was New York.) Whether it was Hollywood politics at play and Rice was purposely passed over, or if he was too late with his pitch is unknown. All we know is that Gentry eventually informed Rice that Matheson was already working on the third story.

Matheson recalled to *The Night Stalker Companion* author Mark Dawidziak that he was surprised to get the call considering the falling out between McGavin and Curtis. "I wasn't sure they'd work together again. But ABC wanted a third Kolchak movie and Dan wanted to do it."[1]

series may not have followed. Just as *Night Strangler* wasn't as good as *Night Stalker*, *Night Killers* looked to be the weakest link of the bunch.

The story would have begun with the lieutenant-governor of Hawaii on his way to a meeting at the Ridgeway Atomic Power Plant when an accident occurs. Kolchak would describe the incident as, "An unforeseen accident that ripped the top right off a Pandora's Box of secrets, cover-ups and murders unlike anything the Aloha State had ever seen."

The Lt. Governor, is rushed to a hospital, and while in the O.R., an explosion rocks the building! We would then cut to a bar in New York, where a drunken Kolchak is regaling another reporter with tales of his far-out adventures: vampires in Las Vegas, a mad scientist in Seattle...

The bartender interrupts Kolchak's rant to tell him that he has a call. "Phone call? Who knows I'm here?" Kolchak asks.

"Your psychiatrist, maybe?" the bartender responds.

Kolchak takes the call to find Tony Vincenzo on the other end of the line, who has been calling "every bar in New York" looking for him.

"Why? What's up?" Kolchak would ask and then we would cut to him mid-flight on the way to Hawaii. All in all the script is off to a good start with a dynamic, mysterious opening, followed by a humorous re-introduction to poor Kolchak.

We get some more clues as to the story while Kolchak reads a current newspaper on the death of the Lt. Governor. But, what catches Kolchak's eye is a smaller news blurb on a UFO sighting in the area.

By the next scene, Vincenzo is driving Kolchak around Hawaii and the duo are already arguing about Kolchak wanting to cover the UFO story rather than the Lt. Governor's death. We also learn that the owner of the paper Vincenzo is working for is the same one that fired the duo earlier in Seattle. Specifically, this one is owned by the editor's playboy son, Elbert Crossbinder, and Vincenzo was hired to help whip it into shape.

Though this dialogue really has no bearing on the plot, it needs to be recounted for fans of that classic Kolchak and Vincenzo banter. Kolchak asks where Crossbinder is and Tony replies, "Africa. Hunting elephants."

Kolchak looks at Vincenzo's stomach. "Speaking of elephants... what have you been eating?"

"Food, Carl, food!" Vincenzo retorts. "My stomach's had a field day away from you."

The android in "Mr. R.I.N.G." Kolchak: The Night Stalker © 1974 Universal Television

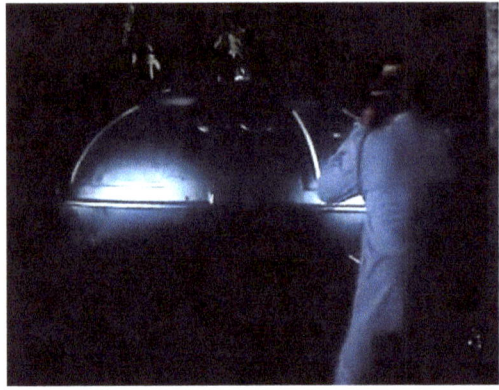

Kolchak photographs a UFO in the episode "They Have Been, They Are, They Will Be..."
Kolchak: The Night Stalker © 1974 Universal Television

The next scene is set in Crossbinder Sr.'s office, where the old man tells Kolchak, "At last, you've reached a locale where that suit of yours is in vogue."

Kolchak smiles and Crossbinder adds, "In beach bum circles."

And yet, Crossbinder still has faith in Kolchak's ability as a reporter, but stresses that he wants him to cover more down-to-earth stories, which most certainly will not include UFOs.

However, the story of the Lt. Governor's death doesn't prove to be as "down to earth" as Kolchak thought. The lone survivor of the O.R. explosion has suddenly died, which gets Kolchak's suspicions tingling that a conspiracy is afoot. Vincenzo, of course, hates this and it gives him stomach spasms.

As Kolchak's investigation continues, he meets Kathy O'Kileyani, a real estate agent. However, she really doesn't add much to the story other than being the movie's obligatory female lead/sidekick for Kolchak. She does this by serving as Kolchak's guide since he is unfamiliar with the island.

The investigation somehow leads to Kolchak being jailed, which

naturally just about does Vincenzo in and also earns Kolchak a trip to Crossbinber's office. Later, things intensify when Kolchak witnesses the murder of a nurse. Kolchak himself is then almost run over by a truck that he saw at the nurse's murder site. Kolchak then goes to investigate the Ridgeway Atomic Power Plant. This proves to be the last straw, and Crossbinder removes Kolchak from the Lt. Governor story and has him investigate the UFO—which is what Kolchak wanted to do in the first place.

With his gal pal realtor as his guide, Kolchak is introduced to Mr. and Mrs. Groat, a couple who saw a "doughnut" shaped UFO land in the vicinity of Hickam Field. Next up, Kolchak interviews one Colonel Shaw, which doesn't really serve any purpose other than to introduce the character so that he doesn't come from out of nowhere later in the story.

The story has a very *X-Files* vibe, naturally, and when Kolchak goes to investigate the UFO landing site, he's shocked to find that the area is off-limits. It's been fenced off via the Spencer Construction Co. Kolchak makes arrangements to interview one of the workers, but the man is killed shortly after. Kolchak glimpses the red truck that he often saw when he was investigating the death of the Lt. Governor and speculates that the two stories must be linked!

Kolchak interrupts Vincenzo in the middle of a golf game to tell him of his theory, which naturally enrages him. (Kolchak's interrupting of the game has also cost Tony a shot and $50 to a competitor in the process).

As was typical of the Kolchak formula, the intrepid reporter goes to visit an old archivist who manages to help Kolchak connect the dots. He explains to our hero that all the spouses of the deceased have also since perished or disappeared. Furthermore, the spot that the UFO landed on was bought by the Spencer Construction Co., but it was the recently deceased lieutenant-governor who brokered the deal.

Kolchak's realtor friend flies him over the landing site in a helicopter (don't ask) and Kolchak encourages her to land. When Kathy expresses a fear of "little green men," Kolchak retorts that he'll just "step on them."

The chopper lands, and it doesn't take long for the duo to spot the UFO. Inside of it they can see figures moving about and the duo deducts that they must be aliens.

Then comes along the red truck that's been tormenting Kolchak for the entire script. It tries to hit the duo but crashes instead. When Kolchak goes to inspect the body he discovers that it's an android.

With the threat revealed, it's now time for Kolchak to get in big trouble before the final showdown (which also happened in the previous two movies). Kolchak and Kathy are arrested for trespassing, and after this, Kolchak does his best to warn Cross-binder, Vincenzo, and Colonel Shaw about the aliens.

"Suppose a space vehicle came to earth carrying, say, half a dozen aliens intent on establishing a base here on Hawaii," Kolchak begins his theory. "They land near Waimea Bay, making the landing site their initial base of operations. Suppose, in order to achieve their goal, they start replacing people with androids—

It's at this point that Kolchak gets cut off and yelled at again. Kolchak keeps pleading with the men that they need to stop an upcoming meeting at the Ridgeway Atomic Plant. Kolchak fears many of the delegates may get turned into androids there. This gets Kolchak fired and he's booted out of the office.

To his horror, Kolchak discovers that even the police chief is an android! Kolchak realizes this when the chief's body begins to smoke and he blows up.

Kolchak: The Night Stalker
© 1974 Universal Television

Kolchak did eventually tangle with aliens in the episode above.
Kolchak: The Night Stalker © 1974 Universal Television

The proposed movie's ending was a doozy—not the good kind either. Kolchak breaks into the Atomic Power Plant to warn the delegates there of the aliens' plan, only to discover the men have already been replaced with androids! Kolchak must then escape them, and somehow he gets his hands on a machine gun and mows the androids down. They all explode, Kolchak saves the world (for now), and he is then carted away by the real authorities.

The story ends with Kolchak's story silenced, because Colonel Shaw doesn't want to risk a nationwide panic. Kolchak's end summarization of events would have gone like this:

KOLCHAK
What worries me though is: what's to prevent those aliens from landing somewhere else; starting in again -- replacing prominent men; taking over? [CAMERA MOVES IN CLOSE ON KOLCHAK] How do we know it isn't happening at this very moment?

Dan Curtis was warm to the script, but Darren McGavin wasn't, which was the first step in terminating the project. Supposedly, in early February ABC was still pondering producing it sans McGavin, but later that month they decided they didn't want to risk replacing the actor. And so *The Night Killers* was kyboshed. Instead, a Kolchak TV series would be produced without Curtis.

Ultimately, I think it's for the best that *The Night Killers* went unproduced. As stated earlier, it had the potential to kill the franchise, and a TV series following this would have been unlikely.

Furthermore, though Kolchak's facing down a lone vampire and an immortal mad scientist were one thing, Kolchak gunning down half a dozen androids begins to strain credibility!

Still from "Demon in Lace"...or is it from *Demon and the Mummy*?.
Kolchak: The Night Stalker ® 1974 Universal Television

The story was also repetitive, hitting all the same notes and character tropes (an elderly archivist, a female sidekick, etc.).

For the sake of argument, let's say that *The Night Killers* was a hit, and a TV series did follow. Considering that the alien plot at the end of *Night Killers* was left unresolved, could we assume that, perhaps, aliens would have been a reoccurring thread in a Kolchak series? Could Kolchak have predated *The X-Files* in yet another way? We'll never know.

As one further aside in regards to *Night Killers*, Matheson also told Dawidziak that he tried to "talk Dan [Curtis] into making it a number of times."[3] Considering that the project was dead as far as McGavin was concerned, I take this to mean Matheson had hoped to retrofit the script as a brand new Curtis production, free of ties to Kolchak. Again, just my own speculation.

All that said, elements from this aborted TV movie did make their way into the series, which featured aliens in "They Have Been, They Are, They Will Be..." and an android appeared in the episode entitled "Mr. R.I.N.G."

As all Kolchak fans know, the series was sadly cancelled after only one season. In fact, not all of season one's proposed 26 episodes were even filmed (only 20 were). As it was, the ratings weren't as high as ABC would like. Coupled with the fact that McGavin disliked how far-out the series had gotten (he did fight a dinosaur in the final episode) ABC decided to cancel it rather than trying their luck at a second season.

While the unmade episodes of season one and two are a story for another time, there is still more to talk about in regards to Kolchak movies. Would you believe me if I told you there actually were two more Kolchak TV movies? Think I'm over exaggerating that statement? Well, you're right... kind of.

Universal, which owned *Kolchak: The Night Stalker* when it came to syndication rights, wanted to get

Darren McGavin guest starring opposite David Duchovny in *The X-Files*.
The X-Files © 20th Century Fox Television

some more mileage out of ol' Carl. They did so by editing two episodes from the series together into a two-hour time slot TV movie. This wasn't exactly unique, as the *Planet of the Apes* TV series did the same thing, but, in the case of the *Kolchak* movies, members of the cast were called in to loop new dialogue.

As the episodes were meant to stand alone, some dialogue had to be altered in order to bridge certain scenes. Not only was McGavin called in for new lines, but so were the actors who played Vincenzo and fellow reporter Ron Updyke (Simon Oakland and Jack Grinnage, respectively). Again, keep in mind they didn't shoot any new scenes, these were just new lines to be dubbed over old ones.

The first two episodes to be stitched together, not unlike the Frankenstein monster, comprised of "Demon in Lace" (episode 16) and "Legacy of Terror" (episode 17). Both episodes involved heart problems. In one, healthy young men suffered heart attacks (thanks to a succubus), and in another, people's hearts were being cut out (thanks to an Aztec ritual). Other than that, there were no ties between the standalone episodes. The results were noticeably choppy and disjointed.[4]

The second of these movies combined "Firefall" (episode 6) and "The Energy Eater" (episode 10). The odd bedfellows in this movie included an invisible Native American bear monster and the fire-starting ghost of a symphony conductor! For this one, at least two new shots were added in. One was a simple insert of a newspaper, and another used old footage to make a new composite shot of Kolchak looking into the sky to see the conductor's giant, ghostly head.

The new edits were done in March of 1976, and thus, two "new" Kolchak movies were born: *Demon and the Mummy* and *Crackle of Death*. The movies and the series both did well in syndication on late night TV. This is probably where the Kolchak TV series really caught on, and also why it has remained on air for many years since (how many other one-season shows managed to do that!?)

As to the downside of the compilation films, they resulted in the episodes that made them being removed from Universal's syndication package. As such, for a time, those were "lost episodes" for Kolchak. In later years, the movies were booted out, and the episodes were re-instated. So, today, both movies are now "lost films" as they never received VHS or DVD releases.

Kolchak's renewed success on cable led to rumblings of a Kolchak reunion movie in the 1990s. Actually, reunion sadly wouldn't have been accurate, as the great Simon Oakland had passed away in 1983. If any of the other Kolchak characters, like Ron Updyke, were going to return is unknown.

Dan Curtis was open to the idea, and so was Darren McGavin, who went so far as to say that he'd do several movies of the week, but not a whole series as he was by now "too old and fat" to do it weekly.

And so Curtis hired Steve Feke, a writer on his current *Dark Shadows* revival, to do his Kolchak revival. The year was 1991, and the story was eventually titled *The Return of the Night Stalker*. It would have seen Kolchak, still down on his luck and arriving in New York. There he begs a job out of Tony Vincenzo's son, an uptight Harvard Business graduate. Soon, strange murders begin taking place. The victims are drained of all blood. Kolchak investigates only to find that the body of Janos Skorzeny (the Vegas vampire from *Night Stalker*) was never cremated! Off Kolchak goes to Las Vegas to investigate... and that's all we know. Dan Curtis said of the project that, "It's the same thing. Nobody believes Kolchak. It's wild. It's funny."[5]

Sadly, the script was never picked up by ABC, and the closest we ever got to a Kolchak revival was McGavin's guest spot on *The X-Files* (originally as Kolchak, but changed

Kolchak: The Night Stalker © 1974 Universal Television

to a different character late in the development). As such, this means that the last time the great McGavin played Kolchak was when he went in to loop a few lines for the awful 1976 TV compilation films!

By 1995, Curtis was trying to remake *The Night Stalker* as a feature film with a new, younger actor playing Kolchak (it was a remake, after all). The *Hollywood Reporter* reported on the project on the front page of its December 12, 1996, issue. Among the interested parties to play Kolchak was Nick Nolte. However, only a few months later, in February of 1997, Dan Curtis's partner in the production, Morgan Creek Productions, pulled out of the picture. Curtis looked for a new production partner, but sadly *The Night Stalker* went quietly into the night. Unfortunately, the only revival we ever saw was the ill-received 2005 *Night Stalker* TV series that aired on ABC.

[1] Dawidziak, Mark. *Night Stalker Companion*, pp.89.

[2] Ibid.

[3] Ibid, pp.90.

[4] I saw these movies as a kid before I knew that they were compilation movies. As I thought that they were real movies, I thought it very strange how both had different plots running at once!

[5] Dawidziak, Mark. *Night Stalker Companion*, pp.192.

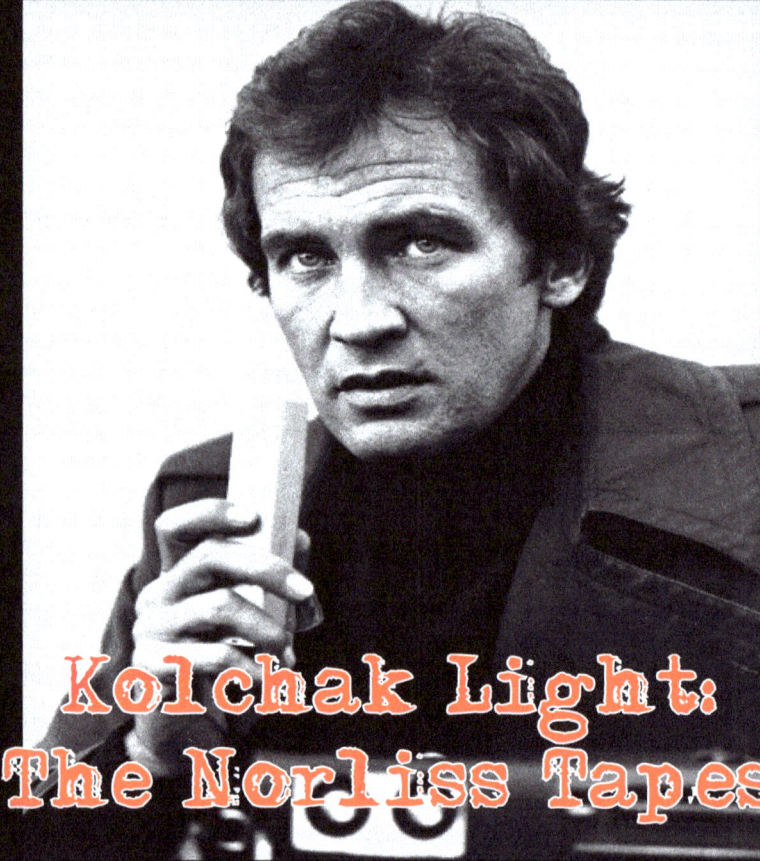

Kolchak Light: The Norliss Tapes

By the time that filming had concluded on *Night Strangler*, Dan Curtis had realized he loved the Kolchak concept, but not Kolchak himself. And so Curtis decided to essentially copy the formula with a new writer character. Curtis even planned for the character to star in a weekly series. This is incredibly ironic since, according to Curtis, ABC approached him to work on the *Night Stalker* series, but he turned them down because he thought it couldn't be done on a week to week basis!

If anything, he probably didn't want to work with McGavin again, hence creating a new but similar character for his own week-to-week

series about a writer dealing with the supernatural.

Curtis got *Night Killers* writer William F. Nolan to write the script, which was based upon a story by Fred Mustard Stewart. Reportedly, Nolan only used the idea of a walking dead man from the story, and all the other ideas were his own. The short story was apparently simply titled "Demon," but Curtis retitled it *The Norliss Tapes* (*Night Stalker's* original title was *The Kolchak Tapes*).

I was rather shocked by this film's existence until I read about it in Mark Dawidziak's *Night Stalker Companion*. I found the film available on YouTube and gave it a watch. I was stunned at just how closely it resembled the two Curtis produced Kolchak films. It has Robert Cobert's same music, it revolves around a vampire draining victims of blood, and it even brings back Claude Akins as another sheriff character trying to cover up the killings! (He played a sheriff in *Night Stalker* too).

However, while it may appear to be a Kolchak copycat, some interesting things are going on in *The Norliss Tapes*. For starters, our main character David Norliss (*The Invader's* Roy Thinnes) is a skeptical writer famous for debunking supernaturalism and mysticism.

As the film starts, we learn that he was hired one year ago to write the definitive book debunking the supernatural. When his editor checks in on him he's shocked to learn that Norliss hasn't even started on the book—or, at least not that version of the book. On the contrary, Norliss has discovered that the supernatural is very real, and he's recorded all of his findings on tape. He sets a meeting with his editor, but then never shows. The editor goes to Norliss's home to find him gone. He notices the tapes though, and pops one in.

And then the movie really begins. At first it's just like *The Night Stalker*, as Norliss narrates his investigation into a series of killings wherein the victims' blood has been drained. His main lead is a widow, Ellen Cort, who claims that the walking dead man is her husband, James Cort.

She reveals that James, an artist, began seeking the aid of an occultist named Madame Jeckiel as he became increasingly ill. Jeckiel (Vonetta McGee of *The Great Silence* and *Shaft in Africa*) gave him an old Egyptian ring with mystic properties. Once Cort died, the ring

resurrected him, but not necessarily as a vampire. The blood is being drained from Cort's victims to make a special clay. Out of the clay he sculpts a body for an evil deity which he intends to bring to life! (Obviously, that's pretty far off from *The Night Stalker* and has more of a save the world vibe to it that Kolchak's adventures didn't.)

Through an arcane ritual, Norliss manages to stop the evil being from incarnating itself. Back in the present, the tape finishes and the editor removes it from the cassette player. He looks at it thoughtfully and pops in tape #2, which would have been episode #2 had this backdoor pilot been picked up for a series by NBC. Presumably, this would have been the format for each week's episode. The lingering mystery of the series may have been the question of where Norliss disappeared to.

The Norliss Tapes was reportedly embraced by Kolchak fans who had yet to see the *Night Stalker* TV series (which had yet to be released) when it aired on February 21, 1973.

The air date is important, as this was around the same time that the *Kolchak: The Night Stalker* series was developing. Obviously, Curtis really wanted to beat ABC to the punch with this series, which would air on NBC.

The movie was well received when it aired, though I'm not sure what kind of ratings it garnered. However, if it had been high-rated then surely NBC would have picked it up for a series.

For years *The Norliss Tapes* was a lost film until it was released on home video in 2006 via Anchor Bay. That DVD is by now out of print, but the movie can be found online. It has since garnered a small cult following.

Tarzan Escapes © 1936 MGM.
Tarzan is a registered TM of
Edgar Rice Burroughs, Inc.

THE CAPTURE OF TARZAN

A TALE OF TWO TARZANS (AND VAMPIRE BATS)

Today it is not uncommon for a completed movie to go before a test audience to gauge reactions only to be totally reshot when said audience reaction isn't what the studio heads wanted. Typically all movies will get re-edited a bit due to audience feedback, and a few additional scenes might be shot to fill in the blanks. But we're talking about when over 50% of the entire film gets reshot, often by a new director. The best example of this in recent years was when *The Avenger's* Joss Whedon reshot most of Zack Snyder's *Justice League*.

One of the earliest examples of this happening was the way that 1935's *The Capture of Tarzan* transformed into 1936's *Tarzan Escapes*. A screening for preview audiences in late 1935 proved to be too intense for theatergoers. The main point of contention was a scene involving giant vampire bats in a swamp. Mainly, the scene terrified children, which caused the mothers in the audience to complain. The disastrous screening, in which children ran screaming down the aisles, has become the stuff of Hollywood legend. Actually, the event might be nothing but a legend, and it may not have even happened, but we'll discuss that later.

Disastrous 1935 test screening or not, *The Capture of Tarzan* was reshot in 1936 to become *Tarzan Escapes*. To backtrack, MGM committed to a third Tarzan movie in 1934 after *Tarzan and His Mate* became a huge hit that same year. The project started life as a treatment entitled *Tarzan Returns* written by Karl Brown in January of 1935. It served as the genesis for the finished film, and included Jane's cousins coming to Africa to look for her. In *Tarzan Returns* they are less sympathetic than the characters presented in *Tarzan Escapes*. The plot in both *Return* and *Escapes* revolves around a search for Jane, who needs to either be proven to be alive, or declared legally dead, in order to sort out a rich uncle's inheritance. If Jane is alive, she gets part of it. If she's dead, the cousins get all of it. See where this is going?

The story's next iteration was called *Tarzan and the Vampires*, as MGM wanted to utilize a horde of rubber bats that it had created for *Mark of the Vampire* (1935). It was a decision that would come back to bite the studio...

The film began shooting in July of 1935 under the title of *The Capture of Tarzan.* Sadly, the footage relating to the original *Capture of Tarzan* has all been lost. But, thanks to a cross promotion tie-in book, we actually do know the original story of *Capture of Tarzan.* Happily, for the Whitman Big Little Book Version of *Tarzan Escapes* the publisher was sent the

MGM's "TARZAN ESCAPES"

In *The Capture of Tarzan,* the lovers lived in a cave rather than a tree house.
Tarzan Escapes © 1936 MGM. Tarzan is a registered TM of Edgar Rice Burroughs, Inc.

original shooting script for *Capture*, not *Escapes*! Thanks to an old article from *ERB Zine* that published the book in its entirety we can now delve into the secrets of *Capture of Tarzan*...

While *Tarzan Escapes* begins with cousins Rita and Eric Parker arriving at the docks of an African village, *Capture* begins with them traveling up river in canoes. The fact that Eric and Rita are unlikable snobs is set up immediately. While the native guides row them across the river, Rita is serving Eric lemonade while a phonograph plays music.

A second canoe holding their luggage comes up beside them. The Skipper in charge of the men suggests that Rita turn down the music lest they attract "unwanted attention" in this "hostile territory." Rita ignores his request, stating,

"Put on another record, Eric. It's his job to make a dull country seem exciting, otherwise there wouldn't be jobs."

As she says this, the beat of jungle drums begins and a spear finds its way into the skipper's shoulder. The canoes beach themselves on an island, and soon, a whole fleet of hostile natives comes around the river bend. A fight ensues where Rita shows her proficiency with a rifle. Eventually, the party is saved by Captain Fry, who has his own native regiment. The dying skipper tries to warn Eric not to trust Fry, but dies before he can get the words out.

Fry takes the cousins back to his camp where he's been trapping animals (one of them is Tarzan's chimp pal Cheetah). Rita makes note of how Cheetah seems accustomed to humans, and Fry mentions rumors of a tribe of "human-like baboons" he's seeking (this being a reference to Tarzan and co.). Eric and Rita explain that they are in Africa to find Jane Parker because they need proof of life for an inheritance (the wicked Rita wants to prove Jane is dead so that she can get the inheritance, which is certainly not the case in *Tarzan Escapes*).

Rita mentions receiving letters explaining that Jane chose to stay with Tarzan the jungle man, which piques Fry's interest as he intends to capture Tarzan.

That night, Tarzan sneaks into the camp to free Cheetah and the other animals. This happens in *Escape* too, but at nearly 30 minutes in, so Tarzan's introduction would seem to come sooner in this version.

Tarzan successfully gets away with Cheetah, and in the aftermath of the breakout, Rita and Fry make a deal to track Tarzan together for their mutual benefit.

In *Tarzan Escapes*, Tarzan returns to a treehouse where Jane is sleeping unaware that he's been away. In *Capture* she is aware of Tarzan's mission and is excitedly awaiting his return alongside a gorilla, Timbee. When she sees Tarzan coming in the distance, she hugs Timbee around the neck. Though this sounds interesting, for whatever reason, *Tarzan Escapes* featured no significant scenes of the Ape Man interacting with gorillas like the previous films did.

Though it doesn't take place in a treehouse, the scene where Jane questions Tarzan about the white men in the jungle is basically the same—not word for word, the dialogue is quite different, but the gist of it is there.

Tarzan shows Jane a picture of her that he found in the camp and she realizes that these must be "her people." When Jane becomes emotional Timbee comes to investigate. Following this is a comical scene where Cheetah steals Jane's photo, and Timbee gets it back for her.

After a great deal of begging, Tarzan reluctantly agrees to take Jane to the encampment. As in *Escapes*, Fry's expedition makes the perilous climb towards the Mutia Escarpment. Jane and Tarzan watches the expedition from the trees. As Jane struggles to see their faces, something tragic happens. Nimba, one of Tarzan's ape friends, is in a tree above Rita. Out of curiosity, Nimba reaches out for her. When Fry sees this he shoots the great ape dead.

A furious Tarzan attacks Fry while Jane shouts at him to stop (while upset, she realizes the party viewed Nimba as an attacking animal and didn't know any better). In the middle of the struggle, Fry aims his rifle at Tarzan and Jane swings from a vine until she lands on Fry, causing him to miss. It's too bad this idea was cut, as it gave Jane the chance to do something heroic.

Jane manages to diffuse the situation, explaining that Nimba was their friend and meant no harm. Fry apologizes, and Jane finally recognizes her cousins. Rita is rather cold, but Eric is delighted to see Jane. When he embraces her Tarzan steps in to stop it, not understanding that they are family, which Jane explains. Though not very affectionate towards Jane, Rita seems to make an effort to flirt with Tarzan.

As in *Escapes*, Tarzan makes it known that he dislikes Fry, though Jane eventually gets him to shake his hand. The awkward situation is broken up when one of the natives is struck by a poison dart. Upon inspection by Tarzan and Fry's

Metro Goldwyn Mayer
El rey de la selva acosado por una tribu de gabonis

This image appears to be of Tarzan fighting the Gaboni in *Capture of Tarzan.*

Tarzan Escapes © 1936 MGM Tarzan is a registered TM of Edgar Rice Burroughs, Inc.

guide, Bomba, the duo determine that the vicious Gaboni tribe is coming.

Tarzan and Jane take to the trees to lead the Gabonis away, while Fry's party runs towards a cropping of rocks to hide. When the Gabonis prove too much for Tarzan to handle, he lets out his signature cry. Soon Timbee and the apes come to his aid and frighten away the Gaboni (that, and Tarzan delivers a death dealing kick to the witch doctor's neck).

Tarzan and Jane regroup with the expedition to discover Rita unconscious from a poison dart. Reluctantly, Tarzan escorts them to his home where there is medicine that can save her. The members of the expedition is flanked on its sides by the apes in what would have been a fun visual.

The apes come in handy when they ward of the Gabonis for a

second time, and then they help to carry the wounded up the escarpment. One of the great apes, wounded from a poison dart, falls from the escarpment while carrying a wounded safari guide. (Some of the guides fall from the escarpment in *Escape* too, but no apes, as there are no apes in *Escape* to speak of).

The next peril to face the expedition is a pride of lions that Tarzan and Timbee ward off together. Some added assistance comes in the form of some elephants which help ward off the big cats. (Notably, Tantor is identified by name in this book version, too).

The group eventually makes it back to Tarzan's abode, which in this version is a cave rather than a treehouse (Tarzan and Jane do have a bed in a tree, the cave seems to be for company). Rita has recovered thanks to medicine administered by Tarzan.

As by this time a swimming scene between Tarzan and Jane was part of the MGM series formula, such a scene takes place in *Capture* too. It's different from the one in *Escapes*. In *Escapes*, Tarzan and Jane's swim is a sort of goodbye as Jane is going to London (this is not the case in *Capture*). A baby deer gets stranded on a log in the water and is attacked by a crocodile. Tarzan saves the animal via a replay of the crocodile scene from *Tarzan and His Mate*.

There is no mention of a crocodile in *Capture's* version here, but such a scene does come into play later. Here Tarzan saves a baby animal, but that's it. Furthermore cousin Eric comes along for the swim in *Capture*.

By this point, Eric's image has softened and he's a sympathetic character. Rita and Fry watch him swim with Tarzan and Jane. In regards to Tarzan, Fry remarks, "I heard somewhere the body of a giant goes with the mind of a child. I was wondering if it applied in this case?"

This lobby card for *Tarzan Escapes* actually features the scene from *Capture of Tarzan* where Rita is struck by a dart. © 1936 MGM Tarzan is a registered TM of Edgar Rice Burroughs, Inc.

Several scenes from *Capture,* such as Tarzan misinterpreting Jane and Eric's hug (right); Tarzan carrying Rita, (bottom left); Tarzan, Jane, and Fry meet the pygmies (page opposite).

Tarzan Escapes © 1936 MGM Tarzan is a registered TM of Edgar Rice Burroughs, Inc.

"So was I," Rita says with a devious smile…

Down below, Cheetah causes mischief and falls into the water where a crocodile tries to make a meal of her. Tarzan doesn't wrestle the croc, though. Instead, he kills it with a spear. (I find it doubtful that this scene was shot. If it was, why not use it in *Escapes* rather than reuse a scene from a previous film?)

Back up top, the conspiring between Rita and Fry continues. Both decide that capturing Tarzan and taking him back to civilization could be even more lucrative than her uncle's inheritance (which she might have to split with Jane anyways). Rita decides to pretend to still be ill from the poison, in a hope that this will prompt Tarzan to lead them back to civilization. The evil ploy works like a charm and off the group goes. (Before he leaves, there's a notable scene of Tarzan addressing the apes, who are sad to see him go, even if only for a few days).

Taking a route that will bypass the Gabonis, Tarzan and co. trek through a murky swamp. Rita, forgetting she's supposed to be sick and only semi-conscious, jolts up and screams. A huge vampire bat is circling the group. It lands on one of the natives and envelopes him like a shroud as he screams and sinks into the mud. Tarzan and Bomba rush to the man's aid and stab the bat to death (though the man is already dead).

Tarzan holds up the ugly creature and several of the characters specifically call it a "vampire" rather than a "giant bat" or "vampire bat" (perhaps this was done in case MGM decided to title it *Tarzan and the Vampires*).

Soon a swarm of the giant bats besets the group, and one even lifts Jane off the ground! The group fights off the giant vermin best they can, but are only saved by the intervention of a benevolent tribe of pygmies. (Since they couldn't get real pygmies, they were played by children in the film).

The friendly pygmies ward off the bats with torches and Tarzan explains they were taking a shortcut to evade the Gabonis. The pygmies also hate the Gabonis and agree to help.

The pygmies show them out of the swamp, and unfortunately, the only way out is across a precarious rope bridge. Though it can support the weight of the pygmies, it seems doubtful that it can support the full grown adults. Tarzan carries the "sick" Rita across first. Then, one at a time, everyone else follows. Jane and Eric are the last to cross when the bridge finally snaps, sending them both careening into the water.

A depressed Tarzan sits by the waterfront while Fry tries to persuade him to continue on with the group, but he refuses. While he's distracted with worry over Jane, Fry seizes the moment to capture Tarzan by having Bomba bash him across the back of the head.

Meanwhile, Jane and Eric survived going down the waterfall, but now must fight off an onslaught of crocodiles. The duo make it to safety and begin constructing a raft to take down river.

Tarzan has been placed within a cage, and as he is loaded onto a steamer with other trapped animals, Rita finally shows some remorse. Lucky for Tarzan, it's Jane and Eric to the rescue, who have climbed aboard the boat to free him. When Fry aims to shoot them all, Timbee comes to the rescue and stops him. It's not just Timbee, all

Tarzan Escapes © 1936 MGM. Tarzan is a registered TM of Edgar Rice Burroughs, Inc.

**More deleted scenes from *Capture:*
Tarzan tied up on the steamer; Tarzan
and Jane ride elephants; and another
shot of the pygmies in the swamp.**
Tarzan Escapes © 1936 MGM Tarzan is a registered TM of
Edgar Rice Burroughs, Inc.

film, the issue of the inheritance is
left unresolved here, or at least it's
not mentioned). Tarzan and Jane
wave to the departing Eric.

"Jane — happy?" Tarzan asks.

"Jane — happy," she responds and
the picture ends.

This version of the film was shot
over 90 days by director James
McCay. Studio heads were
reportedly impressed by the
bat scene and little else.
Much of November of 1935
was then spent discussing
how to fix the film.

From what I'm able to piece
together, MGM felt the film
was too dark and not family
friendly enough in general.
Another point of contention
was the fact that Jane saves
Tarzan at the end instead of
the other way around. As it
was, the entire script was
rewritten by Cyril Hume.
(Even though I prefer the
story of *Capture*, to his credit,
Hume did invent the famous
treehouse that debuts in
Escape and would become a staple
of the series).

Rita became a sympathetic
character in this version, only Fry
was the villain now. A new comical
relief character was added in the
form of actor Herbert Mundin.
Though most of the original cast
returned, there were a few actors
who didn't. According to *ERB Zine*
#618, Granville Bates played the
"boat captain" and Everett Brown
played Bomba (Darby Jones played
him in *Escape*).

James C. McKay refused to do the
excessive reshoots and so was fired.
He was replaced by several
directors for *Tarzan Escapes*, those
being John Farrow, George B. Seitz,
William A. Wellman, and Richard
Thorpe (the only one of the bunch
to receive credit). Notably, John

the apes are there to help Tarzan. In
the chaos, the steamer crashes into
the river bank and catches fire, so
Tarzan must work hastily to free the
captured animals aboard. Rita flees
but is killed by one of the apes,
while a crocodile gets the escaping
Fry in a canoe.

In the epilogue, Eric says a tearful
goodbye to Tarzan and Jane on his
way back to civilization (unlike the

Farrow and Maureen O'Sullivan began seeing each other during the shoot and were later married.

The film started its massive reshoots (really they were filming an entirely new movie based upon the same story) in July of 1936. MGM execs were reluctant to let go of the bat scene and it effectively became the new climax of the movie. What we don't know is how much of the bat scene was reshot to include the new actors: namely Everett Brown and Herbert Mundin.

Maureen O'Sullivan didn't remember the scene kindly either. "It was an awful, disgusting scene," she remembered. She was doubly insulted by the fact that, not only were they not allowed bathroom breaks while filming it, but they didn't even use it! "At the end of the thing, oh, I was furious! Then they cut it from the film so it was all a waste...I would have thought they'd loved it, but they didn't."

As it turns out, reports that the bats caused great consternation at a 1935 preview would seem to be false. It was actually a 1936 test screening where this occurred.

You see, though MGM had exclusive film rights to Tarzan, the Burroughs estate did still lease rights for serials. In 1935 was released *The New Adventures of Tarzan*, which unlike the adult-aimed *Tarzan and His Mate* was made for children. Thanks to that film, Tarzan was now considered kid stuff, hence parents freaking out about the giant bat scenes that were meant for adults in *Tarzan Escapes*.

The fact that the bats were in the 1936 version is backed up by MGM's advertising campaign for *Tarzan Escapes*, which prominently featured the bats.

After the test screening, MGM scrambled to remove the bats. The murky swamp scene still occurs, but

instead of the vampire bats all we get to see are some terrifying iguanas... which aren't the least bit terrifying if you know what an iguana is. They never really interact with the cast. You simply see them slip into the water, and then Fry seems to get pulled under by them somehow! This is similar to Fry's fate in the initial script at least, where he's pulled under by a crocodile.

Despite all the production drama, the film still turned a profit, but due to carrying the budget of two films was not as profitable as it should have been. And what of the vampire bats? Are they gone for good, like the giant spider in the original 1933 *King Kong*?

Well, we're not sure yet. You see, remarkably, a version of *Tarzan Escapes* with the bats was screened in 1954 on a double-bill with *Tarzan, the Ape Man*. Was this a mistake? Was the original exhibited by accident? Apparently not, because ads for the film promised bats the size of vultures attacking Tarzan.

You see, by the 1950s, standards for kid's entertainment had changed, and the terrifying bats of yonder were no longer so scary. Also, it is thought that the original print of *Escapes* was the cleaner of the two to work with for the re-release, which was another reason why it was chosen.

Actually, this reissue didn't just include the bat scene, it also had an extra scene of Tarzan fighting a lion (in fact, stock footage from *Tarzan and His Mate*). It also has a deleted scene where the Gaboni fire blow darts into the foreheads of several of Fry's men.

Ron Hall is one of the more notable historians to have seen this reissue, as he has written several

GIANT VAMPIRE BATS SWEEP DOWN ON THEIR LOVE NEST IN THE TREE TOPS!

NEW THRILLS - NEW ADVENTURES IN THE AMAZIN
TARZAN ESCAPES JOHNNY WEIS
MAUREEN O'

TARZAN ESCAPES

TARZAN ESCAPES New! Tarzan Es

JOHNNY WEISSMULLER
MAUREEN O'SULLIVAN — M-G-M

GIANT VAMPIRE BATS ON MAR
AND IN LOBBY WILL STOP 'EM

articles about it as well as his efforts to figure out where this footage is today. Sadly, by the time *Tarzan Escapes* began showing on TV in the 1960s, the bats had mysteriously vanished. Nor did they resurface on the first VHS release, or the first DVD release. And today, we are still waiting.

Currently archivists are still scouring the MGM vaults for the lost bat footage. So far, nothing has been found. And that's just the bat footage from

Escapes, keep in mind that the print for *The Capture of Tarzan* may have been destroyed back in the 1930s. Back then the historical significance of a "lost film" wasn't recognized. Like *King Kong's* famous "Spider Pit" scene, the whole movie might have simply been destroyed.

So, while chances of *Capture* ever popping up are slim to none, the uncut version of *Escapes* could surface thanks to export prints made by MGM for territories outside of the U.S. Time will tell…

Tarzan Escapes © 1936 MGM. Tarzan is a registered TM of Edgar Rice Burroughs, Inc.

Orca © 1977 Dino De Laurentiis Company

DER KILLER-WAL

mit
Richard Harris
Charlotte Rampling

Regie:
Michael Anderson

A TALE OF TWO SEQUELS

In the middle of the night in 1975, Luciano Vincenzoni, a producer for Dino De Laurentiis, got a phone call from his boss. An excited Dino had just seen *Jaws* and wanted to jump on the aquatic horror bandwagon. He told Vincenzoni to find him "a fish tougher and more terrible than the great white."

Vincenzoni found him *Orca*, a novel about a killer whale who seeks revenge on the fisherman who killed his mate and unborn calf. The book was written by Arthur Herzog, author of *The Swarm*. The film adaptation was faithful to the novel aside from changing the main character's name and a few other minor details.

There are conflicting sources as to *Orca's* budget. Some estimate it to have been as low as $6 million while others claim that it cost twice that much. Despite the respectable reputation it has today, when initially released, *Orca* was labeled

as a *Jaws* knockoff to the chagrin of the cast and crew. *Orca*, though encouraged by *Jaws'* success, was a completely different animal, if you'll forgive the pun. *Orca* succeeded at what *Jaws: The Revenge* would do years later and fail miserably at.

Unquestionably, *Orca* offered a compelling story. It's a story that would have been badly tainted if Dino had made the desired sequels to the film. Yes, despite the fact that *Orca* was not a huge hit (it's estimated to have grossed $15 million) when released in 1978, Dino wanted sequels. And why did he wants sequels?

Well, for starters, *Jaws 2* was on the horizon and poised to be another hit (it was). Secondly, since Dino had already spent money on the Killer Whale animatronics, the sequel would cost much less to produce. This is also why Dino was trying to fast track a sequel to his 1976 *King Kong* remake, he wanted

Eventually Dino had to give up on attempts at *King Kong vs. Orca*. The reason why, for very complicated legal reasons, was that

to re-use the expensive props and animatronics before they degraded.

And speaking of Kong, Dino's first insane sequel pitch—which I still love, by the way—was for *King Kong vs. Orca*! Think it's just internet hearsay? Think again. Numerous sources spoke of the project, and even Dino's wife, Martha De Laurentiis, didn't exactly deny the project's existence when asked about it during an interview conducted for the special features on the Umbrella Entertainment Blu-Ray for *Orca*. (She did agree, however, that it was a crazy idea).

"So if I were to think in Dino's mind," Martha De Laurentiis began, "that *King Kong* was very successful for him... that *Orca* was successful. So, in his way, he's always trying to think, 'What can I do to make another monster movie?'"

How would the two titans have come to blows? Nobody knows. If anything, it was just a title suggestion more than a story suggestion.

Universal had recently acquired film rights to Kong.[1] Sequels to Dino's Kong would have to be approved by Universal. As Universal had released *Jaws*, they were not keen on *Orca*. So there were two strikes against the prospective sequel from the onset.

More developed was the concept Dino had for "Orca Part II" which he approached *Piranha* director Joe Dante to develop and direct.

I discovered this fact via a quote from Joe Dante in the wonderful book *Just When You Thought It Was Safe: A Jaws Companion.* Dante stated that, "*Piranha* had gotten me a picture at Dino DeLaurentis' that I didn't make called 'Orca 2,' about the killer whale — they actually wanted to make a sequel to that! Luckily, it didn't happen, so when it died, I was hired to do 'JAWS 3, PEOPLE 0' instead!"[2]

Unfortunately, information on *Orca Part II* was scarce. For a while, I was worried that was all I would have to go on. But, thankfully, Dante

Had Orca returned for a Part II, his killing spree would have extended onto land!
Orca © 1977 Dino De Laurentiis Company

talked about the project on Gilbert Gottfried's *Amazing Colossal Podcast* on February 8, 2016. The portion of the interview where he talks about *Orca Part II* is, in a word, hilarious. "After I did *Piranha* I got a lot of offers for aquatic movies...I worked with Dino De Laurentiis briefly on *Orca 2*," Dante began the conversation. And then he started to imitate the Italian producer. "And Dino says, 'Orca is a crazy he's a gonna kill everybody!'" This caused Gottfried to laugh uncontrollably at Dante's spot on Dino impression.

Dante continued on that, "Orca was going to go on land and kill people and leave seaweed at the crime scene." Again raucous laughter from Gottfried and his co-host. "This actually didn't strike me as a particularly viable idea. I managed to talk him out of it."[3]

Considering that the first *Orca* was a revenge movie about avenging a dead mate one could compare it to *Death Wish*, which De Laurentiis produced. So I have to wonder, did Dino want to make Orca the Charles Bronson of the seas? Who, or what, was Orca going to avenge next? I wouldn't have been terribly surprised if the idea was that Orca was going to attack all mankind either for ecological reasons (animals attacking mankind for polluting the earth was a common staple of "animals attack" films) or if he singled out mankind for hunting whales. Or, maybe the grief-stricken whale had cracked since the last movie? Or, crazier still, maybe he got a new mate who was also killed by a whaler? (Hey, Charles Bronson's new girlfriends were always getting whacked in the *Death Wish* sequels!)

Like *Jaws*, *Orca* was not a film that needed a sequel. In fact, many people believe that the final shots of *Orca*, of the titular character swimming under the ice sheets, was meant to imply that Orca was committing suicide now that his mission had been finished. So not only was *Orca* supposed to be dead according to some, but bringing the whale back for more revenge would

Some excellent box-art for a VHS release of *Orca*.
© 1977 Dino De Laurentiis Company

His thought process was probably that with Orca you weren't safe in the water or on the land. I'm sure that had the film gotten made there would have been a play on *Jaws's* "Just when you thought it was safe to go in the water..." tagline.

I also have to wonder just how far on land Dino intended the whale to get? Dante mentions that finding seaweed at the crime scenes would be a plot point. If Orca had merely waddled up onto a beach and bit someone in half, the seaweed probably wouldn't be that big of a deal. You expect to find seaweed on a beach.

Actually, though rare, some killer whales do come onto land to catch their prey. According to an article by Damian Wroclavsky on *Science News*, there is only one pod of killer whales in the world that hunt this way, and they hail from off the coast of Patagonia.[4] These whales essentially swim full bore towards the beach at sea lion pups reclining on the shore. The speed propels them to slide onto land capturing the pup in its jaws. The orca will then wiggle itself back near the water in hopes of catching a wave that will help propel it back into the sea.

have undercut the original film badly.

And then there was Dino's way of going about it. Going back to Dante's comment, "Orca was going to go on land and kill people and leave seaweed at the crime scene," it's no wonder Gottfried burst out laughing. I take the original *Orca* pretty seriously and yet even I get visions of Orca sneaking onto land in a trenchcoat and murdering someone in a dark alley. As dumb as it sounds, I think I get what Dino was going for, though. He desperately wanted to one-up *Jaws*.

[1] In the mid-70s, Dino and Universal had competing Kong remakes in development. Dino won that battle, but in later court rulings the Merian C. Cooper Estate finally acquired legal ownership of Kong. Cooper's heirs sold Kong's film rights to Universal, while they retained print rights.
[2] Jankiewicz, Patrick A., *Just When You Thought It Was Safe: A Jaws Companion*, Kindle Edition.

[3] https://www.gilbertpodcast.com/1494-2/
[4] Wroclavsky, Damian. "Killer whales bring the hunt onto land." SCIENCE NEWS, April 16, 2008 https://www.reuters.com/article/us-argentina-orcas-feature/killer-whales-bring-the-hunt-onto-land-idUSMAR71901420080417

Bo Derek lets out a scream in *Orca.* © 1977 Dino De Laurentiis Company

In all earnestness, if this was Dino's idea, it's actually quite terrifying. I can see it now. Some unsuspecting soul walking towards the water's edge, letting the tide run across their feet when—Bam!—Orca shoots out of the water to grip them in his jaws. It actually could have worked. And that would have given the franchise a one-up on scares compared to *Jaws*, where the shark most certainly would not come up to the beach.

I also would not have put it past Dino to set the movie someplace where there are lots of canals. Places within a city that Orca could potentially swim and grab unsuspecting locals and tourists... Venice, perhaps?

There is one other angle to consider about Dino's idea. Though myself and others take *Orca* seriously, there are quite a few people that consider the film to be high camp. Dino may have realized this and decided to just run with it, hence his hiring of the self-aware director of *Piranha*, who quickly acknowledged in his own film that yes, it was a quasi-parody of *Jaws*.

Whether he fought King Kong or came on land to murder people, as much as I love Orca, I think it's for the best that no sequels were produced.

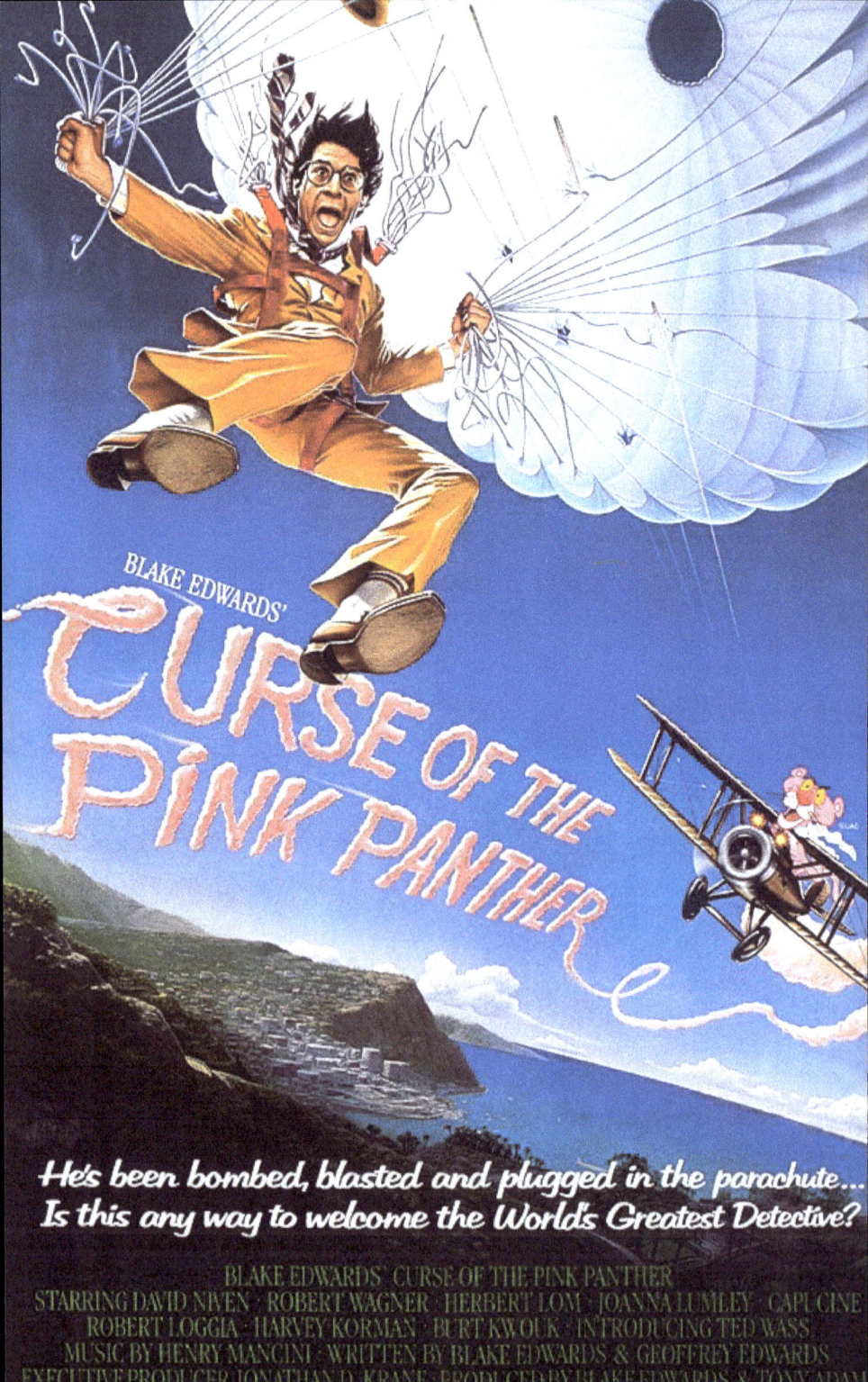

Herbert Lom as Dreyfus was one of the only good things about *Curse of the Pink Panther.* © 1983 MGM

CURSE OF THE PINK PANTHER
Director: Blake Edwards *Script*: Blake & Geoffrey Edwards *Music*: Henry Mancini *Cast*: Ted Wass (Sgt. Clifton Sleigh) Herbert Lom (Dreyfus) Joanna Lumley (Countess Chandra) David Niven (Sir Charles Lytton) Capucine (Lady Simone Lytton) Robert Wagner (George Lytton) Leslie Ash (Juleta Shane) Burt Kwouk (Cato) *Release Date*: August 12, 1983 *Runtime:* 109 Minutes

When it comes to the Pink Panther franchise, there are several entries that could be labeled as the "red-headed stepchild" of the series. The first was 1968's *Inspector Clouseau,* which replaced Peter Sellers with Alan Arkin in the title role. The early 1990s also saw Roberto Benigni playing the *Son of the Pink Panther*. Some might even consider the Steve Martin lead remakes to fall under the red-headed stepchild category. But, unequivocally, the true stepchild in the Panther family is 1983's *Curse of the Pink Panther*. Though the other aforementioned films tried to recast Clouseau, more or less, *Curse* did something completely different in that it tried to replace Clouseau with another character! The plan, in fact, was to relaunch the entire series with a new character, which did not go as planned...

The 1970s saw the release of three very successful *Pink Panther* sequels from the team of director Blake Edwards and star Peter Sellers. 1980 was supposed to see the release of the final Panther film, *Romance of the Pink Panther*, written by Sellers himself. In the story, Clouseau trails a master thief codenamed the Frog, which turns out to be a beautiful woman whom Clouseau marries in the end!

Tragically, Sellers died right before shooting was set to commence. Two years later was released a compilation movie of sorts in the form of *Trail of the Pink Panther.*

Despite Sellers passing, both Edwards and MGM/UA wanted the

43

series to continue, but both had differing ideas as how to do so. MGM wanted to film *Romance of the Pink Panther* with Dudley Moore as Clouseau. (Moore was originally intended as the title star of an aborted Panther spin-off *The Ferret*). Moore, however, would only agree to do the film on two conditions: it would be a onetime gig and Edwards would direct. Edwards felt that no other actor could play Clouseau though, and so the idea to film *Romance* was abandoned in favor of continuing the series with a new character.

MGM/UA reluctantly agreed to this idea of continuing the series with a new character, but felt there needed to be a transitional film to bridge the gap before this happened, and so the idea of *Trail of the Pink Panther* was born wherein cut footage of the deceased Sellers' work would bring Clouseau to life once more.

Edwards then created a plan to film *Trail* and the sequel back to back. The sequel was titled *Curse of the Pink Panther*, which was the original title for what was eventually christened *Revenge of the Pink Panther* back in 1978. In the case of deciding on this name for Panther #8, this title ironically ended up being somewhat prophetic.

When *Curse* was in pre-production, Edwards pondered who could play the new series lead/Clouseau stand-in Sgt. Clifton Sleigh. Edwards again approached Dudley Moore, who rejected the offer based on the fact he didn't want to be committed to a series. Edwards suggested then relatively unknown British comedian Rowan Atkinson, which UA foolishly turned down. Next up, John Ritter was discussed for Sleigh before Edwards eyed *Soap* alum Ted Wass,

whom he felt possessed a certain vulnerability needed for the part. Wass accepted the role and Edwards had his prospective new star for the continuing series.

Amazing as this may sound in hindsight of this film's failure, Edwards actually signed Ted Wass on for six films as Clifton Sleigh! Furthermore, Terry Marcel (second unit director on this film and *Trail*) was already slated to direct the potential first sequel (one of which would come out every three years) while Edwards' son Geoffrey, along with Sam Bernard, would script. The plan, in Edwards's mind, was to continue the Pink Panther franchise with a new lead as though it were the comedic equivalent of the James Bond series.

In this new version, or what today would be considered a reboot, the series would have shifted from France to the U.S., specifically to New York. Lt. Palmyra (played by Pat Corley in the film) would have become the new Dreyfus and Charlie (the African American cop played by Joe Morton) would have taken the place of Francois. Cato, Dreyfus and Balls were to be retired from the series after the release of *Curse*, and the series would have become something more akin to the *Police Academy* movies. In a sense, Edwards was trying to use the Panther brand as a springboard for an entirely different franchise. To imagine the Panther series without not only Clouseau, but Cato and Dreyfus as well, is unthinkable.

As stated earlier, *Curse* was filmed simultaneously with *Trail of the Pink Panther* so as to utilize many of the same actors (some of whom, like Joanna Lumley and Graham Stark, appear in both films in different roles). *Curse* had a budget of $11 million and is clearly the more elaborate of the two. It is also sadly a huge waste of money due to being terribly unfunny as a whole.

MGM already felt that Edwards was spending too much money on the film and had little faith in it. *Curse of the Pink Panther* also has the sad distinction of being the final film of David Niven, who receives top billing. In his autobiography Robert Wagner writes about the filming:

In the spring of 1982, we went to France to shoot *The Curse of the Pink Panther*, which Blake Edwards put together as a last hurrah for the series. Niv played his old part, I played my old part. It was just a couple of days of shooting, but we all wanted to do it for David. After he did his last scene, he said, "I'm afraid you've just seen the last of an actor who had quite a career." Tears came to my eyes.[1]

Like its sister film, *Curse* came in $1 million over budget. To top it all off, it grossed only $4 million at the box office during its late summer release. Amazingly, this would lead to a nearly $1 billion in lawsuits between Edwards and MGM/UA! First, due to *Trail's* failure at the box office, MGM bumped *Curse* from its prime summer spot in May of 1983 back to the last weeks of August with minimal advertising. As this bump in scheduling was technically a violation of Edwards' contract, he used this as grounds to sue MGM for $180 million the following month after release for "willfully sabotaging the film." The next year MGM responded by suing Edwards for alleged fraudulent over-spending. Edwards responded by suing MGM for defamation of character. Eventually, it was all settled out of court by 1988.

And just what went wrong with this film? Well for starters, let's take a look at the story. *Curse* picks up right where *Trail* left off (which revealed Clouseau to be stranded on a tropical island while on the trail of the Pink Panther diamond). Clouseau finds the diamond in the possession of the mysterious Countess Chandra, who becomes enamored with him.

As this is unknown to the rest of the world, who still ponder Clouseau's whereabouts after his disappearance, it is proposed that perhaps the world's greatest detective could be used to find Clouseau. A computer program is set to deduce just who this greatest detective is, but a fearful Chief Inspector Dreyfus sabotages it to recruit the world's worst detective. The incredibly inept Sgt. Clifton Sleigh of the NYPD is selected, and off he goes on the trail of Clouseau to the delight of his tormented co-workers, happy to be shed of him.

Sleigh interviews the likes of Cato and Professor Balls, but it is Sir Charles Lytton, rumored to be the Phantom, who points Sleigh in the right direction and tells him Clouseau was last on his way to Valencia, Spain. There, Sleigh runs afoul of a mob boss trying to kill him, and is rescued by the mysterious Juleta Shane. Juleta is rendered unconscious by a mysterious assailant, and Sleigh must go on the run from the law, who have been informed by a meddling Dreyfus that Sleigh is an impostor.

Sleigh is rescued by George Lytton, and he and his uncle Sir Charles take Sleigh with them to an island housing the estate of the wealthy Countess Chandra. There Sleigh meets Chandra and her lover, who resembles actor Roger Moore (in fact Clouseau, who has

Ted Wass as Clifton Sleigh is about have a painful encounter with Burt Kwouk's Cato. Curse of the Pink Panther © 1983 MGM

undergone plastic surgery). Chandra misinforms him that she had met Clouseau one year ago, and that he had stolen the Pink Panther diamond and then altered his appearance through plastic surgery to become another man: Geno Rossi. When Geno Rossi is confirmed to be dead, Dreyfus happily considers the case closed, and destroys any evidence to the contrary.

Meanwhile, on Sir Charles's yacht, Lady Lytton reveals she stole the Pink Panther from Countess Chandra while Sgt. Sleigh served as her distraction. Sir Charles has the Pink Panther at last…

Of all the strange sequels ever concocted to try and continue a franchise, *Curse of the Pink Panther* has to be one of the all-time strangest. As it is, the film is painful to watch for mainstream audiences and is even more embarrassing perhaps for die-hard fans who so love the classic characters trapped in this true embarrassment of a film.

One of *Curse's* only merits, aside from being a curiosity, for true fans exists in solving the mystery of just what happened to their beloved Inspector Clouseau. This key plot

point is in fact addressed in tantalizing fashion by showing the Inspector alive and well in the pre-credits sequence. And nor is he overdubbed by Rich Little again, but Sellers' own voice through the use of archival audio. In the scene we learn that somehow Clouseau has solved the case and tracked down the Pink Panther diamond—just how we never do learn the answer to. He pulls a gun on Geno Rossi (apparently the thief from the pre-credits scene of *Trail*) who is handing off the gem to a mysterious woman (who we later learn is named Countess Chandra). Naturally, Clouseau fumbles his gun, Geno goes in for the kill, and in a surprise move straight out of a Bond film, Chandra kills Geno saving Clouseau, and then turns the gun on the inspector. With that very intriguing opening the credits begin to play, leaving the audience to wonder just what Blake Edwards has up his sleeve. Unfortunately, it isn't much.

The new titles, again by Marvel Productions (yes, it was related to Marvel Comics) are well done, and utilize a computer theme to match a plot point from the film.

Appropriately, a synthesizer is used to further update the Panther theme for the 80s. From here, the film plays out more or less like a more exciting version of *Trail*, as a new character searching for Clouseau has run-ins with all the usual suspects: Dreyfus, Cato, August Balls, Sir Charles, etc. Unfortunately, this new character, Wass's Clifton Sleigh, sinks the film completely. To be fair, this is not Wass's fault, for not only was he miscast but the idea of the character simply isn't interesting. That a young NYC cop could somehow replace Sellers' expertly played aging Clouseau is beyond this author. Whereas Clouseau was believable and relatable in his bumbling, Sleigh has all the charm of a rodeo clown and lacks the psychological complexity that Sellers brought to his role so well. Truth be told, Edwards might have done better to simply spin the series off to Herbert Lom in some

fashion with support from other regulars like Burt Kwouk.

Speaking of Lom, even Dreyfus's new scenes have grown somewhat thin, though he does get a few good bits. One of the best occurs when he tries to blow Sleigh out of the sky with a rocket launcher. Instead the propulsion from firing the rocket blasts him backwards (in his wheelchair) off of a rocky overhang and into the ocean. Dreyfus gets the last laugh of the picture as well, and in the movie's defense it's actually a good one. In the scene, he sets on fire what may or may not be evidence disproving Clouseau's death. He puts the flaming paper in his trash can under his desk, stamps it out, and then proclaims to an open window, "Peace at last." The desk bursts into flames. Sgt. Sleigh and Francois grab the fire hose and Sleigh blasts the already injured Dreyfus out the window into an awaiting pond two stories below.

Robert Wagner, Capucine, and David Niven are all reunited for the first time since 1964's *The Pink Panther.* Curse of the Pink Panther © 1983 MGM

Above: The new Dreyfus and Clouseau? Not quite... Opposite page: Ted Wass and Leslie Ash. Curse of the Pink Panther © 1983 MGM

Burt Kwouk's scenes as Cato are sadly on par with what was seen in the last film. When we first see Cato flanked by two women, we assume he has gone back to running the brothel we saw in *Revenge*, but instead he has in fact opened a Clouseau wax museum in their old apartment. A funny idea overall, and a great excuse to show off the image of Sellers in the film. Through this, Cato gets a very amusing introduction posing as a wax replica of himself as Sleigh, who has broken into the apartment, looks around. Naturally, Cato comes to life to attack him, but the following fight is so obligatory in nature that it is pathetic, both in terms of comic merit and choreography.

Also pathetic are most of the scenes revolving around Sleigh, though a few have their moments. An abrupt mishap with an umbrella is well handled, and Balls's inflatable companion has a certain potential that it still fails to ever realize, even when it becomes filled with gas and explodes when a hitman shoots it—blowing Sleigh out his hotel room window. The scenes with this companion are also overly crude compared to previous films, and one would be hard pressed to imagine Sellers ever agreeing to do said scenes were they written for him.

Sleigh's constant escaping of some mob hitmen is very Clouseau-like, and though the set-ups are good, watching Sleigh survive isn't nearly as interesting as watching Clouseau. To put it bluntly, Sleigh is painfully unfunny, even though several critics have been strangely kind to the character. Sleigh's scenes also demonstrate that the film's failure isn't in Wass's portrayal, but the writers who came up with the material for him: Blake Edwards and his son Geoffrey. The Waldman brothers, credited on the last film due to use of their material cut in *Strikes Again*, supposedly

Curse of the Pink Panther ©1983 MGM

contributed some early ideas to the screenplay, but what exactly is unknown. Some also speculate that a few ideas from the aborted *Ferret* movie also made their way into *Curse.* Furthermore, Sellers's script for *Romance of the Pink Panther*, which had no input from Edwards whatsoever, was leagues better than Edwards' script for *Curse.*

Edwards' goal to make this the comedy equivalent to the James Bond series is commendable in a certain respect though, and the idea is evident in many facets of the film. For one, there is a great deal of globetrotting, with locales ranging from Paris, New York, Lugash, the South of France, and finally Spain. A scene set in Valencia is reminiscent of a similar scene from *Moonraker*, and that film's Bond star Roger Moore's cameo further hammers home the Bond comparison. There is also an elaborate (and no doubt costly) car chase that occurs in the South of France, which is actually exciting and well-staged.

The film brings up yet more continuity flaws in true Panther tradition in terms of its relation to the preceding film. In this case, Sir Charles tells Sleigh that Clouseau came to see him, whereas in the previous film, this is never implied at all. Considering the two films were written and filmed back to back this is curious. Furthermore, though Lumley searched for Clouseau in the previous film, in this one, she has coincidentally found him—only as a completely different character. Thankfully she is at least disguised enough so as not to be confusing. As an interesting aside, the character of Countess Chandra and her relationship to Clouseau was actually lifted from Sellers's *Romance* script, wherein Clouseau trades in his position at the surete to go on a life of crime with his lover, Anastasia. This film ends with Clouseau turning his back on the law to keep the Pink Panther diamond with Countess Chandra. However, in one of the final scenes, when the duo goes to Chandra's vault, they find the diamond missing and in its place the glove of the Phantom.

This end twist also illustrates how the film's many dangling plot threads occasionally get hard to follow as well, and several points have to be assumed on the point of the viewer. For instance, it can be assumed that the Lyttons manipulated Sleigh during his time in Valencia, then used him to distract Countess Chandra so that they could steal the Pink Panther, though none of this is explicitly confirmed.

Though undeniably poor overall, *Curse* does have a few good points. All fans and critics unanimously agree that Roger Moore's unexpected cameo as Clouseau is the film's highlight. Though not the exit that Clouseau deserved, under the circumstances, it works well, and at least on that front, the character goes out on a high note. Also, one can see Joanna Lumley struggling not to laugh at Moore in one of the scenes, something that often happened with Sellers and his leading ladies. Apparently Moore, on a break while filming *Octopussy*, shot most of his scenes in only one take with no rehearsals. Considering this, it turned out rather well all things considered and is a testament to Moore's comedic ability that he brought so well to the Bond films.

The film has one other bright spot in that it gives more screen time to stars from the original film: David Niven and Capucine. Along with Sir Charles and Lady Lytton even comes nephew George played again by Robert Wagner. Together, the trio manages to liven up the final act rather well. There is also a strange sense of irony to this film in terms of its storyline and its production regarding David Niven. It must be remembered that Niven was actually the star of *The Pink Panther* in 1964, with Sellers' Clouseau only serving in a supporting capacity. For *Curse of the Pink Panther*, Niven is again given top billing, and though his screen time isn't high, he gets the last shot of the film. The Phantom, Simone, and nephew George have stolen the Pink Panther diamond at last, closing the series on a positive note, the best that it can, for fans. Niven died shortly before the film's release, and though this film is in no shape or form a tribute to him as *Trail* was for Sellers, the irony is there none the less.

Ultimately, Edwards still defended the film stating, "I look at *Curse of the Pink Panther*, and it's a good film and a funny film. It may not have done with the others did, if it had gotten the proper sendoff – had MGM done what it was supposed to do – it would've done much better."[2]

Still, with all that said, I think it's a shame the film wasn't included in the recent Blu-Ray set from Shout Factory for the sake of completists. As odd as the film is, it's still part of the Panther family and shouldn't be left out in the cold.

[1] Wagner, Robert, *Pieces of My Heart*, pp.283.

[2] Starr, Michael, *Peter Sellers: A Film History*, pp.240.

Bollywood's rather obscure production of *Aadi Yug—Year One* or *The Earliest Age*—is of interest to giant monster and dinosaur fans for several reasons. Dinosaur enthusiasts will find it of interest for being a Bollywood remake of *One Million B.C.* (1940) and its 1966 Hammer remake. Giant monster fans are interested in the film because it illegally borrowed footage from Toho's *Frankenstein Conquers the World* (1965). That film ended with a giant Frankenstein (who vaguely resembled a caveman) battling a horned dinosaur monster, Baragon. In fact, Baragon's popularity in kaiju circles, in addition to the fact that he's front and center in *Aadi Yug's* posters, is primarily why the movie is even remembered today. Not much is known about the film other than that it was produced by Durga

Director: Prasad *Script*: Nadim Bharti & Aslam Allahabadi (story) *Special Effects*: Dahy Abhai Patel *Music*: Vipin – Kishore *Cast*: Mehndi Jamal, Vinay Kumar, Saheen Aman, Narendra, Rafik Khan, Ramesh Goel, Yusuf Khan & Shyam *Release Date*: January 1, 1978 *Runtime*: 106 Minutes

Films in 1977 and released in early 1978.

Our first shot is of a dramatic, red sunrise, with some equally dramatic music in the background. The camera zooms in, nearer to the sun, then back. And then it zooms in again, backs away again… and again. I'm not exactly sure what the director was going for here, but my best guess is that he was trying to emulate the slow opening of *One Million Years B.C.*, which gave us visuals of a harsh landscape before the narrator cut in to tell us what

Title card.

Adam about to awaken from his slumber.

Adam discovers Eve.

Cavemen on the hunt.

Adam as an old man.

was happening.

However, *One Million Years B.C.* at least changed up the scenery rather than zooming in and out of a sunrise. Finally, after close to two minutes, a narrator begins to speak, explaining to us how God created the world (at least that's what I think it's saying, the subtitles are of the broken English variety). After the narrator finishes his spiel, we're suddenly out in space, where a cartoon star whisks across the screen. It comes nearer and nearer until it stops, becoming stationary.

A picture of an animal in a tree appears, and I'm not sure if it's supposed to be the production company's logo or something relating to the story. Whatever the case, the credits begin to play, and the image changes to that of a monkey. Then the title *Aadi Yug* is superimposed over it, followed by "in orwo color." Despite the picture's talk of God earlier, the monkey begins to evolve into a man through various still pictures. And then, despite this hint towards evolution, our first real scene reveals a naked man awakening from a deep slumber. A mist surrounds his general area, and he acts as though this is the first moment of his life wherein he's been cognizant. In other words, he's like the Biblical Adam.

From a cliff, he spots a woman adrift in the sea on a raft that looks like a nest. Though I assume this is probably derived from Hindu mythology, it's also reminiscent of Tara spotting Sana in the sea in Hammer's *B.C.* sequel, *When Dinosaurs Ruled the Earth* (1970). The man trudges out into the ocean and brings the woman back to shore with him. The naked Adam and Eve stand-ins chase each other around until they do what naked people do—though it's only implied, there's no nudity.

When we next see the duo, they are wearing crude Tarzan and Jane type coverings. As they wander the wilderness, they come across an elephant, which chases them up a rocky front. From the top, the duo observes the elephant coming across another elephant: its mate. Just what's supposed to be happening is unclear, but one of the elephants lays down, and the two humans then give a shocked reaction, so I assume it was giving birth. In the next scene, set some time later, the woman has also given birth. Believe it or not, we are now twenty minutes into the movie, and I basically described everything that happened. So be warned, this is a slow one.

What is Adam pointing to?

It's Baragon! Baragon © Toho Co., Ltd.

But anyway, as the camera pulls back from woman and child, we learn there's been more than just a nine-month time jump. There's now a whole tribe of children running amuck! We jump ahead in time again. Now Adam is an old man, like Akoba in *One Million Years B.C.* From a rocky overhang, he watches his sons hunting some wild game. He calls to his wife and then points to something in the distance. As they look on, we see that they are looking at what appears to be one of their deformed sons battling a floppy-eared dinosaur.

And he's fighting a caveman.

Obviously, this is where the Frankenstein vs. Baragon footage comes in. Considering that Frankenstein was dressed like a caveman, it should come as no surprise that someone decided to pass him off as one. The battle, aside from being intercut with the proud parents, would seem to go in the same order that it does in *Frankenstein Conquers the World.* Even the shots of Baragon breathing fire are retained. The scene is scored

Or is it Frankenstein?

Baragon on the lookout.

53

Fearsome caveman!

Cavemen out on the hunt.

Stalking their prey.

Running after their prey.

Eating dinner.

in a lighthearted comical fashion overall, and one gets the impression that Adam's "son" isn't in any danger from the marauding dinosaur.

An interesting edit occurs after the man has escaped the dinosaur. As Frankenstein looks down on Baragon, who can't seem to find him, he lets out a wolf-like howl to attract his attention! This is probably a good point to mention that none of the Toho sound effects are used. All the monster roars and caveman grunts are unique to this cut. The footage is milked for all its worth, with the scene going on for over five minutes. The footage plays to the point where Frankenstein holds Baragon over his head and spins him, but we don't see him break Baragon's neck. The last we see of the man, he's trying to put out the fire he's started. Mom and pop, meanwhile, have apparently become bored and aren't interested in their son's efforts to put out the flames and wander off.

After our big dinosaur scene is over, for a long stretch, the film mostly resembles Hammer's dinosaur-less opus *Creatures That the World Forgot* (1971). Come to think of it, even this film's locations greatly resemble the ones from the aforementioned film. Scenes of the cavemen out to capture their mammalian prey play out like an inferior version of the same scene in *Creatures*. The *B.C.* nods keep coming, as the next scene has the dead animal roasted over a fire and then torn apart ravenously by the cavemen. Actually, considering that we're now over 30 minutes into this film and don't quite know who our protagonist is, that's yet another way this movie mirrors *Creatures*, where we don't meet lead actors Julie Ege and Tony Bonner until fairly late.

Late one night, three evil cavemen sneak into camp to forage for food. One of them, who has distinct, bright white fangs, picks up a small child (presumably to eat him) before he's caught. A fight breaks out, and one of the good cavemen among the tribe manages to fend off the bandits. As he's the only character we've really focused on within the new era (Adam is by now dead we're so far into the future) I assumed he might be the hero. But, before we know it, he's trying to rape a cavewoman bathing in a river!

A rather toothy caveman.

The scene begins with several cavewomen in the water and is probably meant to be this movie's equivalent of a similar scene in *B.C.* Only here the women are naked, and there's no pterodactyl to terrorize them. Instead, when most of them leave, the unnamed alpha male who drove off the marauders sneaks up on the lone remaining woman.

Cavegirls bathe in a river in a nod to *One Million Years B.C.*

Finally, the real hero makes his entrance to save the girl. He and the alpha male get into a fairly well choreographed and entertaining fight. The struggle is interrupted by a volcanic eruption courtesy of the Hal Roache *One Million B.C.*, which, I'm sure you remember, is in black and white while *Aadi Yug* is in color... To compensate, once the eruption begins, both films are tinted sepia. Also, if my eyes didn't deceive me, I believe I saw a few brief shots from Hammer's *B.C.* eruption as well, as some cavemen run to take cover from falling rocks.

Volcano from *One Million B.C.* (1940).

Some more giant dinosaurs come into play via the giant lizards that appeared in Roache's *B.C.*, which we see get swallowed up in the earthquake. During the chaos, the bad guy manages to catch up with the damsel in distress again and abducts her.

An apeman emerges.

This film's version of the Shell Tribe.

The hero and his girl.

The on-location (not stock footage) waterfall.

Two cavemen enjoy stock-footage from...

One Million B.C.

The riverside climactic battle!

While our hero and a friend are off hunting the kidnapped woman and her abductor, the movie finally debuts its first home-made monster. From out of the bushes, an ape-man sneaks up on two women from another tribe and abducts one of them. It's not a full-on gorilla suit, though. There's no mask, and black body paint is applied to the face of the actor. It's probably most comparable to Bigfoot as seen in *The Six Million Dollar Man* from around the same time.

The hero and his friend vanquish the monster by pushing it into the river. They do so in front of the women's fellow tribe members, who invite them back to their cave lair. Presumably, this is this film's version of the Shell Tribe, who are slightly more refined than the other tribe, which we could also consider to be the equivalent of the Rock Tribe since they live in a barren area.

The Shell Tribe (that's what I'm calling them from now on) lives near a huge waterfall. This waterfall isn't edited into *Aadi Yug* from another movie either; it was actually shot on location.

We cut to another scene, following a hunter of the Shell Tribe. Out in the wild, he sights the giant armadillo from *One Million B.C.* Whereas one could argue that the volcanic ash turned the sky sepia earlier when the *B.C.* footage was used, here there is no excuse. We simply cut back and forth between color footage and black and white. The hunter doesn't even interact with the monster, so the whole scene is pointless.

We also check back in on the villain and the damsel, who are accosted by the three marauders from earlier in the movie. A lengthy wrestling match ensues, and the villain is victorious over the other

The obligatory, ending Bollywood dance number.

villains, again. As the story progresses, the villain tames the three cavemen into becoming his lackeys. One night, as the villain tries to rape the woman, she bashes him over the head with a rock. He passes out and dies, and then the three lackeys proceed to follow her around! She's now the new boss.

Back at the Shell Tribe, along the river, there's a slight recreation of the scene where Tumak learns how to fish. After this, the cavemen witness the famous lizard tussling fight from the Hal Roache *B.C.* As to the footage not matching, I finally realized that this movie wasn't just subpar filmmaking; it was also a comedy. So I guess the footage matching really didn't matter all that much after all.

Our hero seems to have forgotten about the damsel in distress he's been chasing and now has a relationship started up with one of the Shell girls. While they're frolicking in the river, one of their fellow tribesmen comes to get them in an agitated state. Something's wrong! They run back to the cave only to find one of the giant black and white lizards from *B.C.* attacking the cave entrance. Our hero leads the attack on the lizard, though a few shots are really of Victor Mature's Tumak. As in *B.C.*— or rather, through *B.C.*—the

cavemen induce an avalanche onto the monster and the day is saved.

And that is the last of the monster stock footage if that's what you're into. The climax of the film greatly resembles *Creatures That the World Forgot* and involves our hero fighting with another caveman over a girl along a rushing river. The sequence is interminably long.

Tumak wins the fight and takes the new girl back to his home with the Rock Tribe. There finally plays out the film's obligatory dance number, which all Bollywood movies must have. Then, the bad guy that Tumak fought earlier comes back with his friends and starts another fight. But then Tumak's ex, who he was trying to rescue in the first place, comes home with her goons (ya know, the ones who attacked the Rock Tribe before) and orders them to save Tumak. The three ruffians beat the bad guys and save Tumak. The End.

As you can imagine, this is a movie to be endured by only the most devoted connoisseurs of Z-grade filmmaking, kaiju enthusiasts, or completests of the caveman film genre. And if you took the time to read this entire article, that just might mean you. It's out there in the interwebs if you wish to see it...

TOM SELLECK PLAYS INDIANA JONES...
AS MAGNUM P.I.

Growing up I always thought that the fact that Tom Selleck was the original choice for Indiana Jones was some sort of secret, arcane knowledge, only recently revealed to the masses.[1] But, apparently it wasn't that secret, especially if you've seen every episode of *Magnum P.I.*

In the 8th season, episode 10: "Legend of the Lost Art" aired on February 10, 1988. Remarkably, the episode provided a beat for beat remake of *Raiders of the Lost Ark* in less than an hour! That's quite a feat in my book. If you didn't know that Selleck was the original choice for Indy (and I'm not sure how many people actually did in the pre-internet age) you might have called the episode a "rip-off" when, in fact, it was an ingenious in-joke.

The episode begins with a man exploring an ancient cave in Hawaii, though we don't see his face for some time. Before we do, the man wards off the usual tropes of bats, rats, and spiders before he can get to his prize: a booby-trapped ancient artifact. In this case, the artifact is an ancient scroll, and the explorer does turn out to be Magnum, who successfully makes it out of the cave alive... eventually. As in *Raiders*, various triggers unleash spears and other projectiles at him, and in the end he has to run out of the cave before it caves in on him.

Magnum returns to the Robin Masters estate where he angrily berates Higgins for sending him on such a dangerous mission. And for making him wear "that hat!" After Magnum hands off the parchment to Higgins and marches out of the room, in sneaks Peter Riddley-Smythe, a double-agent spy who plucks it from Higgins and escapes. Though he's a spy, in appearance and mannerisms, he's modeled after Beloq.

Our next scene recreates the Tibetan cantina scene in *Raiders* by way of Rick's club. There, an old flame of Magnum's who he hasn't seen in several years (à la Marian Ravenwood) is waiting for Higgins. The woman, Connie Northrop, has a prism which can somehow translate the old parchment paper belonging to Higgins. But, before they can pool their resources some bad guys show up to take it. In walks Magnum to save the day and a bar fight ensues with much of the same choreography as the one in *Raiders*.

In the next *Raiders* inspired scene, Magnum watches as Connie is kidnapped by the bad guys and put on a sea plane which explodes. For a moment, Magnum thinks she's dead, but then he remembers that this is just like something he's seen in a movie. You see, throughout the episode Magnum references how the situations they are in reminds him of movies he's seen. However, no one ever once mentions *Raiders* (that film apparently doesn't exist in this universe), instead they mention many of the old films and adventure serials that inspired *Raiders*. Magnum cites an old serial where you think the heroine is dead, but really she jumped to safety at the last moment.

This turns out to be true of Connie too. Magnum (in full Indy regalia now), Higgins, T.C., and Rick sneak into the enemy camp and inside one of the tents Magnum finds Connie alive and well. He rescues her, reacquires the McGuffins they need, and they escape onto their final destination. Going back to the cave from earlier, Magnum and co. find the real room where the "lost art", a secret scroll full of ancient knowledge, is held (there was a subplot earlier about the other script being a decoy that's not worth explaining). Magnum and Connie retrieve the scroll from a buried room that turns out to be full of, you guessed it, snakes. Magnum "hangs a lantern" (that's film talk for asking the audience to ignore a plot hole or something that's a little too convenient) by noting that there are no snakes in Hawaii and then the bad guys show up. They take the scroll, kidnap Higgins, and trap Magnum and Connie with the snakes. As in *Raiders*, Magnum manages to figure out the secret way out of the room and the duo are off to rescue Higgins.

The climax isn't similar to *Raiders* at all, which is understandable considering that *Magnum P.I.* would never get supernatural with ghosts and such. There's a simple gunfight with all the principals (Magnum even uses a bullwhip) and most of the bad guys bite the dust.

The episode ends with a little epilogue where Higgins tries to convince Magnum to go back with him to the cave to find the rest of the "lost art". Magnum shoves him out the door, looks at the fedora rather disdainfully, and hangs it up. He then places his Tigers ball cap back on and all is right with the world.

And yes, you can watch Selleck as Jones in a screen-test on the *Raiders* DVD bonus features, but if you really want to see him in action as Indiana Jones, check out "Legend of the Lost Art."

---

[1] Selleck was the first round pick for Indy, but had to turn it down due to his commitment to *Magnum P.I.* Ironically, an actor's strike then occurred that delayed production on *Magnum P.I.* which would have actually allowed him to play Indiana Jones. Only a few weeks after Spielberg learned Selleck wasn't available Harrison Ford was cast and the rest was history.

MOONLIGHT MASK: THE MOVIE
REMEMBERED
by Connor Anderson

THE MOON MASK RIDER

A SUPER HERO ON A SUPER BIKE NOW ON SCREEN IN A SUPER LIVE ACTION.

From the late 1970's through the early 1980's, many famous tokusatsu properties were getting new leases on life, with varying results. Daiei's *Gamera Super Monster* proved to be the final nail in the coffin for the character until the successful Heisei reboot in 1995. Ultraman didn't find too much success either in this period, as the 1980 incarnation of the show, *Ultraman 80*, didn't fare much better, despite featuring some wonderful special effects and charming stories, leaving the franchise in a strange limbo of theatrical clipshows and failed

foreign productions until 1996's *Ultraman Tiga*. Toei's own *New Kamen Rider* and *Kamen Rider Super-1* felt too similar to the older shows and would never reach the heights of the much different *Kamen Rider Black* in 1987. However, lost in the shuffle of all of these projects, was the comeback of one of Japan's classic heroes from the Showa era; one that predates the likes of Kamen Rider, Ultraman, Super Sentai and all the various transforming heroes in-between. That hero is Gekko Kamen, or Moonlight Mask as he's known in English.

Opposite Page: International poster for *Moonlight Mask: The Movie*. This page: Magazine spread for the new Moonlight Mask (top) and a bizarre scene from the movie (bottom).

While he's not as well known to many fans of tokusatsu here in the West, Moonlight Mask was, as stated earlier, the first ever TV superhero, created by Yasunori Kawauchi in 1958 for the Tokyo Broadcast Station, or TBS. The show featured the title character battling various villains and criminal organizations that threatened Japan, and a multi-episode arc of the TV show even had Moonlight Mask going toe-to-toe with the kaiju Mammoth Kong, a character who is likely the first ever TV kaiju. None of the other characters on the show knew who Moonlight Mask's secret identity was, but it was hinted to audiences that he was detective Juro Iwai, who would disappear right before Moonlight Mask would step in to

save the day. The show was incredibly popular and spawned a multitude of tie-in products and even six theatrical films in the late 1950's. Tragically, Moonlight Mask's acts of heroism on the small screen would inspire kids to imitate their hero, and the series would soon find itself canceled after a young boy leapt to his death while trying to emulate Moonlight Mask. The series would later be revived in the form of a 1972 anime by Knack, the same studio responsible for the infamous and unintentionally hilarious *Chargeman Ken*, as well as the two Go Nagai robot shows *Groizer X*, and *Psycho Armor Govarian*. It's a little surprising that a new tokusatsu version of the

character wasn't around during the Henshin Boom in the 1970s, and that it'd take another decade for the character to enter live-action once again.

Produced in 1981 by Premier International and Herald Enterprises and written by Kawauchi himself, *Moonlight Mask* was intended to be a proper update for the character, bringing him back onto the silver screen in full color. The film's story has a People's Temple inspired cult known as New Love Country, who terrorize Japan by committing all sorts of heists, clad in some stylish red cult robes. Opposing them of course, is Moonlight Mask. Here, Moonlight Mask's secret identity is hinted as being George Ohara, a mild-mannered scientist, rather than Juro Iwai from the original TV program. The film's climax involves Moonlight Mask foiling New Love Country's Jonestown-inspired mass suicide, and battles their leader as he tries to make his escape via helicopter, before riding off after the day has been saved.

While this film was anticipated as the character's big comeback, much like several of the examples seen above, this was sadly not the case. In spite of a massive publicity campaign, the film failed to connect with audiences, with many fans of the original TV show criticizing the changes made to the character and the film not utilizing any of the side characters from the original. The film bombing also killed the career of the new Moonlight Mask's actor, Daisuke Kuwahara, with this being his last major film role. Moonlight Mask himself would once again go into dormancy, only returning some 18 years later in a gag anime that aired in 1999.

Looking at the movie upon retrospective some 40 years or so later, it's easy to see why this film bombed. The movie looks more akin to an episode of a tokusatsu show, rather than a big-budgeted reboot. Despite being only 107 minutes, the film moves at a glacially slow pace, as the story places many of its scenes at the police station, interspacing them with a few action sequences until the finale.

On the subject of the action set pieces, they feel fairly primitive, and aren't as flashy or elaborate as what Toei was doing in their programs at the time with the Japan Action Club, leading to a sense of blandness during moments that should be seen as exciting. The film is also home to some odd moments, and while strangeness is usually par for the course in Japanese hero media, it comes across as fairly forced, and moments that should be memorable, like the remote controlled helicopter stealing a briefcase full of money, or the band that dresses like Moonlight Mask, feel like they were cut from a different film entirely, and don't gel well with the rest of the picture. Needless to say, even with Kawauchi himself spearheading this revival, the end result feels flat and uninspired.

The film isn't without its charms though, and there's some elements to it that are likeable enough. The updated version of Moonlight Mask's outfit for one, is a great rendition of the character's costume, taking inspiration from the 1972 anime incarnation and realizing it well in live-action. It's a shame it appears in a film as drab as this, because it's a great update for the character and just looks cool as hell when the character is speeding along on his motorcycle. While the main villains aren't as threatening as their real-world inspiration (and I for one would've chosen Mammoth Kong for the big reboot, but I digress), the idea of a Jim Jones styled cult leader is a clever and topical foe for this reboot. And while I wouldn't call the film's theme song "MOON MASK RIDER" as good as the openings for *New Kamen Rider* or *Ultraman 80*, it really is a catchy song, and I found myself humming it during my day quite a few times.

1981's *Moonlight Mask*, at the end of the day, is a film that had a lot of potential, but failed to live up to it. Much like many of its contemporaries, *Moonlight Mask* proved to be a dead end for the character in the 1980's. But unlike many works from around that time period, the film doesn't really earn a second look, and it's fallen into a somewhat deserved obscurity. Perhaps one day we'll see a new tokusatsu version of Moonlight Mask, and should we, let's hope it's better than what Premier International and Herald Enterprises gave us nearly forty years ago.

PREVIOUS ISSUE:
THE LOST FILMS FANZINE #1
SPRING 2020 In this issue explore the long lost Italian cut of Toei's 1977 epic, *Legend of Dinosaurs and Monster Birds*. The Italian cut, titled *Terremoto 10 Grado*, completely overhauled the film, re-editing and shuffling scenes, adding in a new subplot, and even rescoring it with the John Barry score from *The Deep* (1977)! Discover the hidden history of the aborted sequel to 1971's *The Abominable Dr. Phibes*, *Bride of Dr. Phibes*, which ended up also becoming the unproduced sequel to 1972's *Dr. Phibes Rises Again*. Learn about Merian C. Cooper's original color vision for his two 1935 epics: *She* and *The Last Days of Pompeii*. Marvel at the Hammer *King Kong* remake that evolved into a Volkswagen commercial! Uncover the Bollywood version of *Jaws*, *Aatank*, which began shooting in the 1980s but didn't wrap until 1996! Then, discover the secret 1967 Toho Godzilla movie which you can watch right now, if you know where to look... This, and more!!!

NEXT ISSUE:
THE LOST FILMS FANZINE #3 FALL 2020
This extra-large monster-sized issue will explore Hammer's classic 1958 opus *Horror of Dracula* uncut. This includes an examination of scripted scenes that went unfilmed, plus footage both lost and found, like the infamous uncut death scene discovered in Japan in recent years. Original versions of *Son of Frankenstein* will be explored, as will unmade and forgotten sequels to *The Blob* (1958). Joey Palinkas charts the development of John Brosnan's *Carnosaur* from a truly epic novel to a not so epic but fondly remembered series of Roger Corman films. *Bride of Godzilla's* 65th Unniversary will be celebrated, plus more surprises that we don't even know about yet!!!

VISIT US ONLINE AT:
https://www.facebook.com/John-LeMays-Lost-Films-Book-Series

CPSIA information can be obtained
at www.ICGtesting.com
Printed in the USA
BVHW090841091220
595258BV00016B/876

9 781734 781663